WOMEN'S
WICKED
WISDOM

WOMEN'S WICKED WISDOM

from Mary Shelley to Courtney Love

Michelle Lovric

CHICAGO
REVIEW
PRESS

Compilation copyright © Michelle Lovric 2003
Design copyright © Carlton Books 2003

Published in 2004 by
Chicago Review Press, Incorporated
814 North Franklin Street
Chicago, Illinois 60610

ISBN 1-55652-540-0

Printed in Great Britain
by Mackays

Contents

I love being an assertive, uppity woman.
What's the alternative?
Erica Jong

I have a snug little taste for impertinence.
Mary Russell Mitford

There are times when a sub-text simply won't do.
Lynne Truss

I love men, but women inspire me.
Monica Bellucci

A great dame is a soldier in high heels.
Marie Brenner

If you want to see the girl next door, go next door.
Joan Crawford

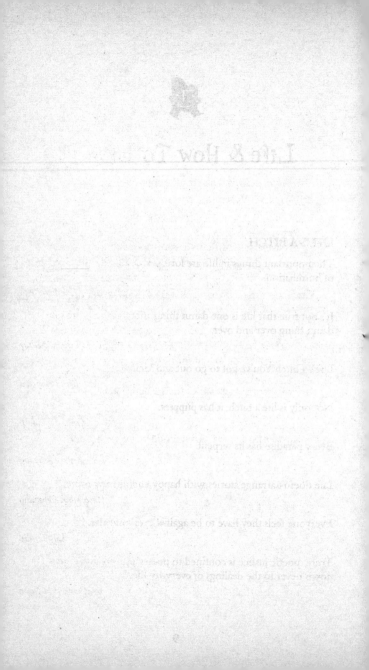

Life & How To Live It

LIFE'S A BITCH

The important things in life are love, sex, death and the avoidance of humiliation.

Sue Townsend

It's not true that life is one damn thing after another – it's one damn thing over and over.

Edna St Vincent Millay

Life's a bitch. You've got to go out and kick ass.

Maya Angelou

Not only is life a bitch, it has puppies.

Adrienne E. Gusoff

Every paradise has its serpent.

Elizabeth von Arnim

Life doesn't arrange stories with happy endings any more.

Rosamund Lehmann

Everyone feels they have to be against everyone else.

Lily Tomlin

Truly, poetic justice is confined to poetry indeed: and comes down never to the dealings of everyday life.

Rhoda Broughton

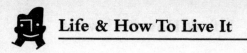

Don't expect such wonders of people – our ancestors were only lately throwing coconuts at each other's heads & swinging by their curly tails.

Isadora Duncan

You're depressed? Of course you're depressed. That's how you know you're awake … Only a moron would not be depressed.

Fran Lebowitz

Life is not fair. Neither is the orgasm.

Susan Sarandon

I am sure the facts of life – the marryings and bearings and buryings are the least important.

Virginia Woolf

What should we do if we had to remain in this world perpetually? We cannot inhabit a house for three days in this miserable world without being dissatisfied.

Giulia Gonzaga

Life is like being given a dartboard, and then being told there's nowhere in the house that you can play darts.

Lynne Truss

I'm afraid consciousness and intelligence do little to help you through life practically.

Rachel Griffiths

Never be so simple as to seek for happiness: it is not a bird that you can put in a cage.

Caitlin Thomas

You come into the world alone and you go out of the world alone, yet it seems to me you are more alone while living than even going and coming.

Emily Carr

We assume we are playing the lead, but turn out to be bit-part players in someone else's drama.

Fay Weldon

Expect the worst and you won't be disappointed.

Helen MacInnes

Things are always darkest just before they go pitch black.

Kelly Robinson

Life is hard. After all, it kills you.

Katharine Hepburn

THE "ME" GENERATION

What this generation was bred to at television's knees was not wisdom but cynicism.

Pauline Kael

Kids are getting cynical earlier and earlier and earlier … pretty soon, I guess, the Muppets will be in bondage or something.

Lily Tomlin

Men seldom risk their lives where an escape is without hope of recompense.

Fanny Burney

Cynicism is not realistic and tough. It's unrealistic and kind of cowardly because it means you don't have to try.

Peggy Noonan

Our own integrity starts eroding, because the standard of what's valued and what's respected is diminished and diminished and diminished.

Lily Tomlin

Whenever people say we mustn't be sentimental, you can take it they are about to do something cruel. And, if they add, we must be realistic, they mean they are going to make money out of it.

Brigid Brophy

Life & How To Live It

It's only a matter of time, when people are negative, and the majority of people are, for us to open things up to an entity, for people like Osama Bin Laden or Hitler ... eventually that's our responsibility. We created it. We created an opening with our desire to "receive for only ourselves" mentality.

Madonna

We are so vain that we even care for the opinion of those we don't care for.

Marie von Ebner Eschenbach

No insect hangs its nest on threads as frail as those which will sustain the weight of human vanity.

Edith Wharton

Millions long for immortality who don't know what to do with themselves on a rainy Sunday afternoon.

Susan Ertz

I used to think formerly that I loved the whole world; but I see that this universal love is only another name for universal indifference.

Marie Bashkirtseff

I would rather be a dupe occasionally, than suspect all the world of selfishness and dishonour; for then my life would be a burden to me.

Harriette Wilson

The two kinds of people on earth that I mean,
Are the people who lift and the people who lean.

Ella Wheeler Wilcox

I very much like working with young people, because they're cunning. They grab what you've got.

Thelma Holt

Instant gratification is not soon enough.

Meryl Streep

DON'T FENCE ME IN

All the world's a cage.

Heanne Philips

I don't exist well in a confined state.

Nicole Kidman

I don't like having time measured by such set horizons so that we cannot help knowing how it goes, or seeing how very little worth anything fills the space between.

Geraldine Jewsbury

I want a wild, roving, vagabond life, I always want to do something daring and spirited; you will certainly repent it, if you keep me tied up.

Isabel Arundell (later Burton)

Bitches seek their identity strictly thru themselves … they never marry anyone or anything; man, mansion, or movement.

"Joreen": The Bitch Manifesto

This is the life many women lead: two paths diverge in a wood, and we get to take them both.

Nora Ephron

I wish I had spent my life with much less fear. I wish I had just had adventures.

Tama Janowitz

I don't want to get to the end of my life and find that I have just lived the length of it. I want to have lived the width of it as well.

Diane Ackerman

GOOD & EVIL

When I first started reading Greek drama, I was so struck by this sentence, I believe from Sophocles: if evil leads to evil where shall the chain of evils end?

Donna Tartt

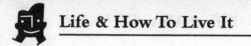

When milk and poison come together, the poison does not become milky, it is the milk which becomes poisonous.

Indira Gandhi

Lead me not into temptation; I can find the way myself.

Rita Mae Brown

I think we're all a mixture of haloes and horns. I know I am.

Dolly Parton

It is common to express surprise at the unprovoked viciousness of Mortal Man, let us sometimes wonder at their unencouraged Virtue.

Hester Thrale

Never doubt that a small group of thoughtful, committed citizens can change the world: indeed it's the only thing that ever has.

Margaret Mead

The people in the parks, the alcoholics, the homeless, they are looking at you. Do not be those who look and do not see.

Mother Teresa

If you stop to be kind, you must swerve often from your path.

Mary Webb

He who never sacrificed a present to a future good or a personal to a general one can speak of happiness only as the blind do of colours.

Olympia Brown

People who know the truth have no business to allow the powers of darkness to silence them on any point that matters.

Marie Stopes

The only thing that scares me more than space aliens is the idea that there aren't any space aliens. We can't be the best creation has to offer.

Ellen DeGeneres

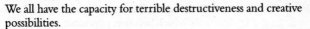

We all have the capacity for terrible destructiveness and creative possibilities.

Annie Lennox

Hopefully we won't blow up the world before we get a chance to find out how we can evolve into a higher species!

Goldie Hawn

TAKING CHARGE

The only difference between a rut and a grave is in their dimensions.

Ellen Glasgow

Seize the moment. Remember all those women on the *Titanic* who waved off the dessert cart.

Erma Bombeck

Posterity is full of men who seized the day, while the women were planning for a fortnight on Tuesday.

Allison Pearson

The secret of getting ahead is getting started.

Sally Berger

Don't agonize. Organize.

Florynce Kennedy

You can't build a reputation on what you intend to do.

Liz Smith

Your playing small does not serve the world!

Marianne Williamson

Do not wait for leaders; do it alone, person to person.

Mother Teresa

You may be disappointed if you fail, but you are doomed if you don't try.

Beverly Sills

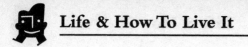
What if? That's the dumbest thing in the world.

Elaine Stritch

Life is about chasing after the things you truly think are worth it, even if they don't happen. I'd rather have nothing but know I didn't settle for something I didn't want.

Salma Hayek

A stale mind is the devil's breadbox.

Mary Bly

It is boredom which slows down time.

Janet Baker

People do not live nowadays – they get about ten per cent out of life.

Isadora Duncan

It's a hell of a thing to be born, and if you're born you're at least entitled to your own self.

Louise Nevelson

Identity is not found, the way Pharaoh's daughter found Moses in the bulrushes. Identity is built.

Margaret Halsey

No one's life is ordinary. We're all the heroes and heroines, with fate or flaws to beat.

Maeve Binchy

You don't get to choose how you're going to die. Or when. You can only decide how you're going to live. Now.

Joan Baez

Submission to what people call their "lot" is simply ignoble. If your lot makes you cry and be wretched, get rid of it and take another.

Elizabeth von Arnim

Life & How To Live It

It is vain to say human beings ought to be satisfied with tranquillity; they must have action, and they will make it if they cannot find it.

Charlotte Brontë

I like people who are pathological about things.

Zadie Smith

Power is the ability not to have to please.

Elizabeth Janeway

It pays not to compromise.

Edith Piaf

There are only two ways of spreading light – to be the candle or the mirror that reflects it.

Edith Wharton

Some people, like padded Oscar Wilde, prefer to be on the inside of society: looking out. But I prefer to be, like skinned Van Gogh, on the outside of society: looking in.

Caitlin Thomas

You cannot shake hands with a clenched fist.

Indira Gandhi

Everyone has inside of him a piece of good news. The good news is that you don't know how great you can be! How much you can love! What you can accomplish! And what your potential is.

Anne Frank

Our deepest fear is not that we are inadequate.
Our deepest fear is that we are powerful beyond measure.

Marianne Williamson

You must do the thing you think you cannot do.

Eleanor Roosevelt

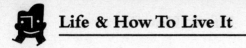

Life & How To Live It

A SENSE OF HUMOUR

We're medically designed to laugh at ourselves because
otherwise we wouldn't be able to fart – if the human race didn't
fart we probably wouldn't have a sense of humour. It's a sort of
design fault.

Jenny Eclair

When humour goes, there goes civilization.

Erma Bombeck

There was so little humour in my childhood; now I am catching
up with it.

Edith Piaf

Humour distorts nothing, and only false gods are laughed off their
earthly pedestals.

Agnes Repplier

If haloes must be worn, they can be worn at a frivolous, becoming
angle.

Renee Long

Wit seems to be like Fire: it will blaze away once it is begun, but it
must first be lighted.

Hester Thrale

There's a hell of a distance between wisecracking and wit. Wit has
truth in it; wisecracking is simply callisthenics with words.

Dorothy Parker

The difference between a clever talker and one who delights in
saying things which embarrass and annoy is much the same as
that which exists between a first-class fencer and a bungling
assassin.

Lady Dorothy Nevill

Laughter is more deadly than vitriol.

Dillie Keane

We hear a lot about the situations our sense of humour has saved.
Not so much about those that it has shot down.

Caitlin Thomas

THE WIT OF WOMEN

There's a great male myth that women aren't funny, but I think
men just don't like what women are funny about.

Kathy Lette

The comedian has to get a laugh from the audience, just the way a
prostitute has to get an orgasm from the client.

Camille Paglia

There is not one female comic who was beautiful as a little girl.

Joan Rivers

I'm not funny. What I am is brave.

Lucille Ball

Stand-up is ninety per cent front.

Jo Brand

The first time I "stood up" was at a cowboy bar in Houston,
Texas. Try being a feminist comic when the entire audience is
chewing tobacky and playing with their firearms!

Leigh Anne Jasheway

People say things about comedy, such as … "It's the most scary
thing in the world." That's rubbish. The scariest thing in the world
is getting killed, being in a nuclear war, getting punched, or getting
raped.

Jo Brand

You get a cocktail of emotions about women who are funny.
Firstly, it's jealousy, but very soon after, you are so glad to be a
punter and to be enjoying it.

Dawn French

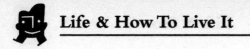

It's hard to be funny when you have to be clean.

Mae West

He who laughs last didn't get it.

Helen Giangregorio

THE ART OF TALKING

Blessed is the man who, having nothing to say, abstains from giving wordy evidence of that fact.

George Eliot

Silence in a woman is a moving rhetoric.

Hannah Woolley

A good listener is not someone who has nothing to say. A good listener is a good talker with a sore throat.

Katharine Whitehorn

There is no such thing as conversation. It is an illusion. There are intersecting monologues, that is all.

Rebecca West

Listening, not imitation, may be the sincerest form of flattery.

Joyce Brothers

No one really listens to anyone else, and if you try it for a while you'll see why.

Mignon McLaughlin

I'm an excellent talker. I've often said that I'd like to have my own talk show – with no guests.

Fran Lebowitz

Good communication is as stimulating as black coffee, and just as hard to sleep after.

Anne Morrow Lindbergh

If someone tells you he is going to make "a realistic decision," you immediately understand that he is going to do something bad.

Mary McCarthy

Cynicism is an unpleasant way of saying the truth.

Lillian Hellman

EXPERIENCE

Never regret. If it's good, it's wonderful. If it's bad, it's experience.

Victoria Holt

Experience: A comb life gives you after you lose your hair.

Judith Stern

Life is made up of moments, small pieces of glittering mica in a long stretch of grey cement.

Anna Quindlen

All the past is not worth one today.

Ella Wheeler Wilcox

What a wonderful life I've had! I only wish I'd realized it sooner.

Colette

In retrospect I rather enjoyed my youth, the only thing I regret about it was that it wasn't sufficiently misspent.

Jilly Cooper

The only thing I regret about my past is the length of it. If I had to live my life again I'd make all the same mistakes – only sooner.

Tallulah Bankhead

The past is your make-up; it is with you, on you, you wear it.

Diane Modahl

I think you reach a point when you reach a certain age when you've had a certain amount of life experiences, where you just go, okay, well this is the journey … And if you keep waiting to be happy, that's never going to happen.

Nicole Kidman

Why, what is to live? Not to eat and drink and breathe, but to feel the life in you down all the fibres of being, passionately and joyfully.

Elizabeth Barrett Browning

When you realize the value of all life, you dwell less on what is past and concentrate more on the preservation of the future.

Dian Fossey

Does not every phase of our life possess its own attractions, riches, and compensations? We must live as we ride; be supple, avoid checking our steed without need, hold the bridle lightly.

George Sand

Fortune … is so fantastic, that there is nothing we may not expect from her caprice.

Marie de Sévigné

If I have learned anything, I owe it neither to precepts nor to books, but to a few opportune misfortunes. Perhaps the school of misfortunes is the very best.

Louise Honorine de Choiseul

To taste life is not to be confused with understanding what life is really all about.

Wallis Windsor, Duchess of Windsor

The prior knowledge of the unpleasant side of life is essential to the proper appreciation of the luxurious innovations.

Caitlin Thomas

We all run the risk of declining, if somebody does not rise to tell us that life is on the heights, and not in the cesspools.

George Sand

A woman's life can really be a succession of lives, each revolving around some emotionally compelling situation or challenge, and each marked off by some intense experience.

Wallis Windsor, Duchess of Windsor

BAD BEHAVIOUR

Whatever you choose, however many roads you travel, I hope that you choose not to be a lady.

Nora Ephron

I always wanted to walk on the wrong side of the road, me, with the traffic coming on.

Julie Walters

To err is human, but it feels divine.

Mae West

As soon as you forbid something, it thrives.

Rachel Stirling

I hope there's a tinge of disgrace about me. Hopefully, there's one good scandal left in me yet.

Diana Rigg

I have been living exclusively on champagne & caviar & dancing the Mazurka with ten young Polish Counts – all of them quite mad.

Isadora Duncan

I have always felt really naughty … I always felt that if someone approached me to try something, then I would be the last person to walk away. I'd have a go.

Angelina Jolie

I once nearly broke Baroness Thatcher's toe at a party on my way to lick David Mellor's ear.

Tara Palmer-Tomkinson

If I have a choice between the very horrible joke and the not so horrible, I'll always go for the very horrible one just because I enjoy that really. I like swearing as well.

Jo Brand

Only good girls keep diaries. Bad girls don't have time.

Tallulah Bankhead

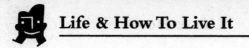

Since when was genius found respectable?

Elizabeth Barrett Browning

If you obey all the rules, you miss all the fun.

Katharine Hepburn

It will be a hideous world when everything is permitted ... We need laws to break in order to give our vitality exercise.

Katherine Mansfield

Good and bad, right and wrong, are as clear to me as sweet and sour, or black and white. But the trouble is that no moral question is either sweet or sour or just black and white. It's often bland and tepid, or grey and tan.

Mae West

Shame is a passion that might be of excellent advantage to us, if we managed it well.

The Marchioness of Lambert

As prudence is the eye of the soul, so discretion is the apple of that eye.

Hannah Woolley

I only regret getting caught. I don't regret anything else.

Heidi Fleiss

I don't suffer very much from guilt.

Joan Collins

The world wants to be cheated. So cheat.

Xaviera Hollander

I've pretty much behaved like a knucklehead my entire life.

Cameron Diaz

I love going out and I love getting drunk, and before it was always like, "Mmm, life gets in the way of my party."

Zoë Ball

I didn't start my company until I was twenty-nine, because I had so much partying to do.

Lulu Guinness

Parents have the idea that it is their duty to set a good example, never realizing that a bad one will do just as well, indeed better.

Jill Tweedie

I am ashamed of confessing that I have nothing to confess.

Fanny Burney

TRUTH & FICTION

As for the truth, I'm quiveringly uncertain of it. Reality has changed chameleonlike before my eyes so many times.

Maya Angelou

The truth will not stay fixed.

Maureen McHugh

I have come to the conclusion, after many years of sometimes sad experience, that you cannot come to any conclusion at all.

Vita Sackville-West

Truth isn't elegant; that's just mathematician's sentimentality. Truth is squalid and full of blots, and you can only find it in the accumulation of dusty and broken facts, in the cellars and sewers of the human mind.

Hilary Mantel

Our ability to delude ourselves may be an important survival tool.

Jane Wagner

Reality is something you rise above.

Liza Minnelli

Facts are not important.

Marlene Dietrich

Imagination and fiction make up more than three quarters of our real life.

Simone Weil

Involuntary error is a calamity. Negligence of truth is more.

Harriet Martineau

People will more readily swallow lies than truth, as if the taste of lies was homey, appetizing: a habit.

Martha Gellhorn

There is no genuine hypocrisy that does not contain a grain of sincerity.

Marie d'Agoult

You should always believe all you read in the newspapers, as this makes them more interesting.

Rose Macaulay

General notions are generally wrong.

Lady Mary Wortley Montagu

History's what people are trying to hide from you, not what they're trying to show you.

Hilary Mantel

Liars destroy the currency of all words.

Elizabeth Jane Howard

Of all lying experts: not excluding the Sicilian or Welsh; the foxwily Solicitor is, without pinch of doubt, the most phenomenal exponent of lying.

Caitlin Thomas

Nobody speaks the truth when there is something they must have.

Elizabeth Bowen

It is useless to hold a person to anything he says while he's in love, drunk, or running for office.

Shirley MacLaine

There is nothing worse than being lied to by someone who isn't putting their heart and soul into it.

Barbara Ellen

ADVICE

The idea of strictly minding our own business is mouldy rubbish. Who could be so selfish?

Myrtie Barker

Why don't you learn from my mistakes? It takes half your life to learn from your own.

Shelagh Delaney

Please give me some good advice in your next letter. I promise not to follow it.

Edna St Vincent Millay

I love getting advice because it is a caring, intimate experience and I always listen openly before deciding if the other person's perspective works for me.

Normandie Keith

There's no such thing as advice to the lovelorn. If they took advice, they wouldn't be lovelorn.

Fran Lebowitz

I have seen myself grow, so I can never again close the door on anyone because he or she holds a position diametrically opposed to mine.

Maya Angelou

I listen and give input only if somebody asks.

Barbara Bush

Nagging is the repetition of unpalatable truths.

Baroness Edith Summerskill

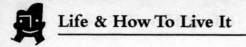

Life & How To Live It

ATTITUDE IS EVERYTHING

If we wish to grow old gracefully we must commence by being young cheerfully.

Marie Corelli

You cannot prevent the birds of unhappiness from flying over your head, but you can prevent them from nesting in your hair.

Dillie Keane

There is nothing more sexy than confidence.

Lynne Franks

Mistakes are a fact of life. It is the response to error that counts.

Nikki Giovanni

I like living. I have sometimes been wildly, despairingly, acutely miserable, racked with sorrow, but through it all I still know quite certainly that just to be alive is a grand thing.

Agatha Christie

When nothing is sure, everything is possible.

Margaret Drabble

Nothing in life is to be feared. It is only to be understood.

Marie Curie

I have discovered that patience is not the ability to wait, but the ability to keep a good attitude while waiting.

Joyce Meyer

Indifference to most of the things that worry, trouble and poison most people is a wonderful lubricant for life.

Vicki Baum

My self-confidence depends on the fact that I have discovered my dimensions. It does not become me to make myself less than I am.

Edith Södergran

I haven't had the humility to find anything beneath me.

Beryl Bainbridge

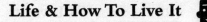

If by nature you are volcanoes, at least be only smouldering ones.

Elizabeth von Arnim

One cannot collect all the beautiful shells on the beach. One can collect only a few, and they are more beautiful if they are few.

Anne Morrow Lindbergh

Knowing what you cannot do is more important than knowing what you can do. In fact, that's good taste.

Lucille Ball

Envy is such a waste of time.

Ira von Furstenberg

The happy people are failures because they are on such good terms with themselves that they don't give a damn.

Agatha Christie

Accept that all of us can be hurt, that all of us can – and surely will at times – fail … I think we should follow a simple rule: if we can take the worst, take the risk.

Joyce Brothers

Pain is good for vitality.

Susan Sarandon

Our feelings are our most genuine paths to knowledge.

Audré Lord

The trouble with life isn't that there is no answer, it's that there are so many answers.

Ruth Benedict

What person in the world goes through life in a straight line?

Gail Godwin

LIFE IN THE FAST LANE

I live with Carpe Diem engraved on my heart.

M. F. K. Fisher

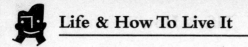

If my life were a car, it would be in fifth gear.

Rosie O'Donnell

I have a hard time staying in the present … My head is always two months down the road.

Catherine Ryan Hyde

There seems to be a general overall pattern in most lives, that nothing happens, and nothing happens, and then all of sudden everything happens.

Fay Weldon

If you realize too acutely how valuable time is, you are too paralyzed to do anything.

Katharine Butler Hathaway

Time granted does not necessarily coincide with time that can be most fully used.

Tillie Olsen

Life today is nervous, sharp and zigzag. It often stops in midair.

Martha Graham

Women used to have time to make mince pies and had to fake orgasms. Now we can manage the orgasms, but we have to fake the mince pies. And they call this progress.

Allison Pearson

I don't get disorientation because I've never stayed in one place long enough to feel odd about leaving it.

Naomi Campbell

Nothing can be really enjoyed at top speed, especially life.

Rachel Ferguson

Events … to which one looks forward with enthusiasm pass away like running water.

Bettina Brentano

I want to walk through life instead of being dragged through it.

Alanis Morrisette

My favourite week in the diary is when there is nothing planned, what I call white time.

Rose Tremain

There is a great lordliness in simplicity, very aggravating to bustlers.

Stevie Smith

DUTIFUL DAUGHTERS

Women … have a duty to keep young. We should live adventurous lives, travel, work hard, earn money, spend it, love someone deeply, have children. That is life.

Helena Rubinstein

Favours are an anchor; favours are a drag.

Irma Kurtz

There are always dues to pay.

Ellen Gilchrist

I don't like Duty – everything in the least disagreeable is always sure to be one's duty.

Elizabeth von Arnim

I always wanted everyone to be pleased with me. I went out of my way to be sweet and loving. It was a value that my family stressed.

Jennifer Lopez

Anybody that's trying to please everyone is going to have a frustrating life.

Susan Sarandon

CURIOSITY

Four be the things I'd been better without: love, curiosity, freckles, and doubt.

Dorothy Parker

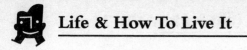

As I live mostly by curiosity, everything in my life starts with a question.

Vicki Baum

Knowing too much is very apt to make us troublesome to other people.

Lady Mary Wortley Montagu

I had Hamlet's disease of introspection. I was always looking for the integrity behind it.

Geri Halliwell

Seeing is seizing, seeing is knowledge, knowledge is control: so cover up!

Fay Weldon

The cure for boredom is curiosity. There is no cure for curiosity.

Ellen Parr

SWEET BIRD OF HAPPINESS

The greater part of our happiness or misery depends on our dispositions and not on our circumstances.

Martha Washington

Happy people are never brilliant. It implies friction.

Katherine Mansfield

Achievement of your happiness is the only moral purpose of your life, and that happiness – not pain or mindless self-indulgence – is the proof of your moral integrity, since it is the proof and the result of your loyalty to the achievement of your values.

Ayn Rand

Unexpected pleasures are the only pleasures in the world.

George Sand

Happiness shouldn't be a goal. It isn't something you can achieve, it's a by-product of what you do.

Dorothy Rowe

Life & How To Live It

When a small child … I thought that success spelled happiness. I was wrong, happiness is like a butterfly which appears and delights us for one brief moment, but soon flits away.

Anna Pavlova

If you haven't been happy very young, you still can be happy later on, but it's much harder, you need more luck.

Simone de Beauvoir

The lovely thing about real happiness is that it is there all of a sudden, unexpected, weightless as a little summer cloud and just as radiant and intangible.

Vicki Baum

Women On Women

DEFINING ROLES

I refuse to be a female impersonator. I am a woman.

Germaine Greer

I've been a woman for a little more than fifty years, and I've gotten over my original astonishment.

Nadia Boulanger, when asked how it felt to be the first woman conductor of the Boston Symphony Orchestra

The natural superiority of women is a biological fact, and a socially acknowledged reality.

Ashley Montagu

Woman is the primaeval fabricator, the real First Mover. She turns a gob of refuse into a spreading web of sentient being, floating on the snaky umbilical by which she leashes every man.

Camille Paglia

Women never have young minds. They are born three thousand years old.

Shelagh Delaney

I've talked to women all over the place at the book signings – Japan, America, Scandinavia, Spain – and what they most relate to is the massive gap between the way women feel they're expected to be and how they actually are.

Helen Fielding

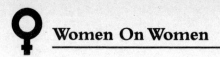

In the past, ambitious women had to pretend to be stupid to be acceptable; now, they must pretend to be complex, traumatized "survivors". In the light of this sexist, miserabilist orthodoxy, surely clear-eyed, hard-hearted happiness is the most maddening subversive weapon a woman can wield. Say cheese!

Julie Burchill

Women seem to me to be divided into two groups – those who reason and those who are for ever casting about for reasons for their own lack of reason.

Wallis Windsor, Duchess of Windsor

Women can go far with very little.

Phyllis Chesler

The glossy magazines further perpetuate the myth of the ideal woman, only now she has to reach new heights of perfection. The ideal woman windsurfs, paraglides, sunbathes in the nude, cooks in a wok, counts kilojoules instead of calories, and has a wonderful way with tradescantia.

Dillie Keane

Woman is the conserver of tradition, but she is also the absorber of the shocks of the future. Therefore, she must be a bridge and a synthesizer.

Indira Gandhi

Though everybody else may distrust women, I understand them perfectly. I do not bother whether they have lied, betrayed, sinned, or whether they have been lost from their birth, once I feel that they have wept and suffered while lying or sinning or loving. I stand by them, I stand for them, and I burrow, burrow into them.

Eleonora Duse

Women in touch with their intuition and integrity hold all the cards.

Jane Lapotaire

Procreation & Pride

BUN IN THE OVEN, MUSH IN THE BRAIN

There's never a reason to have a baby, only emotion.

Fay Weldon

Women's bodies are the first environment for all of us.

Sandra Steingraber

Are you sitting comfortably? Feeling wide awake, tip-top, super-fit, alert? The chances are, if you say yes to all of these and are a woman, you are not pregnant.

Amanda Craig

Giving up nicotine, alcohol, codeine, and caffeine was just the beginning. I would have to get some friends who wore cardigans with jeans that fit, who answered their phones by saying "Johnson residence" instead of "Heartless Bitch Hotline! How may I wound you?"

Lily James

If they really wanted to lower the number of teenage pregnancies, they would pay women who've had a couple of kids to visit secondary schools and demonstrate their varicose veins, stretch marks and piles.

Jenny Eclair

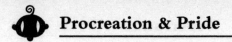

Procreation & Pride

We are supposed to take pregnancy in our stride and not hide it away as the Victorians did, but it's interesting how few depictions of heavily pregnant women exist in film.

Amanda Craig

The Spanish for pregnant may be *embarazada*, but of course expectant mothers feel proud, not embarrassed.

Isabel Fonseca

Children change you too: you absorb their characteristics as they grow in the womb, it isn't all a one-way street.

Fay Weldon

My mother had a good pregnancy in the sense that she didn't know she was pregnant until the day I arrived.

Hattie Hayridge

If pregnancy were a book they would cut the last two chapters.

Nora Ephron

There's no better way of getting acquainted with your own particular form of dementia praecox than by having a baby.

Cornelia Otis Skinner

GIVING BIRTH

Giving birth is like taking your lower lip and forcing it over your head.

Carole Burnett

I want to have children, but my friends scare me. One of my friends told me she was in labour for thirty-six hours. I don't even want to do anything that feels good for thirty-six hours.

Rita Rudner

If men could get pregnant, abortion would be a sacrament.

Florynce R. Kennedy

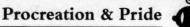

It is unheard of, uncivilized barbarism that any woman should still be forced to bear such monstrous torture … It is simply absurd that with our modern science painless childbirth does not exist as a matter of course.

Isadora Duncan

A lot of women I know believe in natural childbirth. Just thinking about that pain makes me want to take drugs.

Ellen DeGeneres

I've known women who were taking conference calls in the delivery room and who ignored their labour until the midwife turned off their mobile.

Amanda Craig

I am freaked out by the biology. An entire person covered in slime bursts out of your intimate regions, and no one thinks it's strange. This is a Stephen King story, isn't it?

Stephanie Calman

As for Mama, she never recovered completely from the combined shocks of sex and childbirth.

Vicki Baum

If they get olive oil from olives then where the hell does baby oil come from?

Andrea Lemon

BABIES RULE

Babies are born looking like the ugliest relative on his side of the family.

Jenny Eclair

Father asked us what was God's noblest work. Anna said men, but I said babies. Men are often bad; babies never are.

Louisa May Alcott

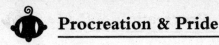
There are many of us who believe that the public breast-feeding of babies big enough to rip open ringpulls with their teeth has more to do with attention-seeking than with animal instinct.

Julie Burchill

Becoming a parent was like trying to build a boat while you were at sea.

Allison Pearson

I hope there is a special angel that looks out for small children because it is an impossible task for anyone without wings.

Elizabeth Forsythe Hailey

MOTHERHOOD

There's a difference between wanting to have a baby and wanting to be a mother. When you're younger, it's all about having a baby. But truly being a mother is so different and carries with it so much more.

Brooke Shields

I always think mothers must give daughters a sense of themselves … I think I would probably have had more natural confidence if I'd had a mother.

Madonna

I remember one of my playmates from around the corner died, probably of leukaemia. My mother took me to this funeral and took me up to see Rachel … and she said, "This is what happens when you don't listen to your mother."

Amy Tan

We are transfused into our children, and … feel more keenly for them than for ourselves.

Marie de Sévigné

I suppose we are all the products of our parents' joy and suffering. Their emotions are written into us, as much as the inscriptions made by their genes.

Siri Hustvedt

Never allow your child to call you by your first name. He hasn't known you long enough.

Fran Lebowitz

The way I saw it, my mother was a goddess, sometimes a cranky one, but a goddess nonetheless.

Cher

As a child I thought I had clever strategies for rebellion, but my mother had even more clever strategies.

Amy Tan

A child judges the whole world by its mother.

Fanny Douglas

Mother doesn't have to be perfect, just consistent.

Nancy Friday

I love my mother, admire her, want to be like her … and then go crazy when I see myself turning into her. I give myself big speeches about the evolved, enlightened adult relationship I'll have with her, and then revert to a five-year-old the second we're in a room together.

Cathy Guisewite

CHILD-ACHE

I'm suffering from "child-ache" – rather like having toothache, or a headache.

Christiane Collange

You can be yourself for maybe your twenties or your teens and there are all these choices. But somehow that only goes up to when you have kids … and then it's back to like the '50s.

Ariel Gore

They're all mine … Of course, I'd trade any one of them for a dishwasher.

Roseanne Barr on her children

Being constantly with children was like wearing a pair of shoes that were expensive and too small. She couldn't bear to throw them out, but they gave her blisters.

Beryl Bainbridge

What I was doing with My Brain these days? … I can only resolve to shelve the entire question until the children are grown-up, when Brain, such as it is, may perhaps come out of retirement.

Rosamund Dashwood

Holding on to your personality is being true to your children.

Ariel Gore

Many people have said to me, "What a pity you had such a big family to raise. Think of the novels and the short stories and the poems you never had time to write because of that." And I looked at my children and I said, "These are my poems. These are my short stories."

Olga Masters

The same woman who may be willing to put her body between her child and a runaway truck will often resent the day-by-day sacrifice the child unknowingly demands of her time, sexuality, and self-development.

Nancy Friday

I suspect that the reason many of us find eating with children tedious in the extreme is that we're too right-on and weedy to crush their little spirits by saying, "You're being amazingly boring."

India Knight

There's a huge difference between being a mother and acting the part of a mother. [In Forrest Gump,] Tom Hanks wasn't really my son, so I didn't have to worry about what he was eating during the day.

Sally Field

There really aren't mommy heroes.

Ariel Gore

My mother would look at me and say, "Great God! What have we reared?" as if I was a heifer.

Julie Walters

Sometimes when I look at my children I say to myself, "Lillian, you should have stayed a virgin."

Lillian Carter, mother of Jimmy and Billy

We spend the first twelve months of our children's lives teaching them to walk and talk and the next twelve telling them to sit down and shut up.

Phyllis Diller

If you feel you must smack your child, do be sure it is because your argument needs strengthening and not just to relieve your own personal feelings.

Judith Martin

If parents behaved less like grown-ups, would young people behave less like little children?

Christiane Collange

Experts say you should never hit your children in anger. When is a good time? When you're feeling festive?

Roseanne Barr

Always be nice to your children because they are the ones who will choose your rest home.

Phyllis Diller

MOTHERS & FATHERS

Mothers are a biological necessity; fathers are a social invention.

Margaret Mead

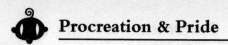

Mother wants what's best for her kids; Daddy only wants what's best for Daddy, that is peace and quiet, pandering to his delusion of dignity ("respect"), a good reflection on himself (status) and the opportunity to control and manipulate.

Valerie Solanas

If it were natural for fathers to care for their sons, they would not need so many laws commanding them to do so.

Phyllis Chesler

When women walk out on their families for five hours on a Saturday, it's called abandonment. When men do it, it's called entitlement.

Susan Maushart

It is taken for granted that every other famous man from Tom Hanks to Nigel Lawson will at some point have abandoned a first family to start a second one. Yet famous Bad Fathers are miraculously few and far between.

Julie Burchill

MOTHER-GUILT

The four basic guilt groups – food, love, mom and work – are still going strong.

Cathy Guisewite

At work, you think of the children you have left at home. At home, you think of the work you've left unfinished. Such a struggle is unleashed within yourself. Your heart is rent.

Golda Meir

My children cause me the most exquisite suffering. It is the suffering of ambivalence: the murderous alternation between bitter resentment and raw-edged nerves, and blissful gratification and tenderness.

Adrienne Rich

The world of women was divided in two: there were proper mothers, self-sacrificing bakers of apple pies and well-scrubbed invigilators of the twin-tub, and there were the other sort.

Allison Pearson

My mother could make anybody feel guilty – she used to get letters of apology from people she didn't even know.

Joan Rivers

Is not the inferiority complex, about which so much is written and spoken, nowadays shifting from the child to the parent?

E.M. Delafield

The women who tell you so glibly that they "have given their lives to their children" probably didn't have much to give.

Renee Long

MAYBE BABY, MAYBE NOT

A fire has been lighted … It all started with the pill, of course. Not because it enabled women to avoid having children … because for the first time in the history of humanity, that decision belonged to women.

Françoise Giroud

I once talked to Tracey Emin about our abortions; I'd had loads more than her, but she couldn't get her head around the fact that they had no more significance to me than having one's tonsils out, while her couple had caused her all sorts of arty trauma and led to the creation of several artefacts. Bless!

Julie Burchill

At my age, women are supposed to hear the loud ticking of a biological clock, but I think I must have bought the wrong batteries for mine.

Lynne Truss

Your career is your favourite child.

Jill Robinson

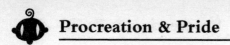

Procreation & Pride

I do not have children. I do have, or have had in previous years, all sorts of advice from strangers impertinent enough to give it, as to why I should have them. Can I claim, as a woman, to feel completely fulfilled? There are innumerable ways for human beings to "give birth".

Janet Baker

What I have I'm glad to have. What I haven't had I can't really grieve about and you can't grieve about a child that's never been born. I think if you had a child that was killed or died or stolen: imagine trying to live with that.

Barbara Taylor Bradford

Now I realize that what I want is a book. So much do I want to give birth to a book that I experience "false alarms" – when I think I am "with book", but am not really. Once a month I phone my agent and say "It's happening!"

Lynne Truss

I'm thrilled that I don't have children. I have the thing that I love, which is freedom. I think having a loving family around you is an essential in life but you can have that without having your own children. Just let other people have the children!

Helen Mirren

The problem is that motherhood is about as fashionable as the puffball skirt.

Gillian Bowditch

I would have made a terrible parent. The first time my child didn't do what I wanted, I'd kill him.

Katharine Hepburn

LETTING GO

Nothing is more beneficial in the treatment of children than a little wholesome neglect.

Fanny Douglas

I've never seen a happy spoilt child or adult.

Ira von Furstenberg

It is a dead-end job. You've no sooner learned the skills than you are redundant.

Claire Rayner on motherhood

The best way to keep children at home is to make the home atmosphere pleasant – and let the air out of their tyres.

Dorothy Parker

I can't help but wonder, is this the same kid I used to spank?

Barbara Bush on her son, President George W. Bush

Only by discarding her children before they discard her, the wise mother knows, will there be a remote chance of their voluntarily visiting her later. Of their even being quite fond of the old trout.

Caitlin Thomas

Where It All Begins

CHILDHOOD

I feel sure than unborn babies pick their parents. They may spend a whole lifetime trying to figure out the reasons for their choice, but nothing in any human story is accidental ... I decided to be a girl.

Gloria Swanson

When I was born I was so surprised I didn't talk for a year and a half.

Gracie Allen

My father whenever I had anything the matter with me always reproached me by telling me that I had been born a perfect baby.

Gertrude Stein

My dad said to me, one Christmas: "You were the ugliest child the hospital had ever seen. When we took you home they gave us two blankets – one to put over your head."

Barbara Ellen

I don't think I remember my first memory.

Ellen DeGeneres

Early memories have, I suppose, something inevitably traumatic in their composition. They record moments of being shocked, pitchforked out of the dream of wake which is our natural infant state.

Rosamund Lehmann

Today's children are reluctant to sleep, in case the world is different when they wake. Everything moves so fast.

Fay Weldon

My mother was a social worker. Naturally we were very disturbed children.

Jo Brand

My mother was an earthbound angel, which may have been the reason Pop was a scamp.

Anita Loos

The mind of the child resembles that of the artist inasmuch as nothing appears to it as finite.

Edith Sitwell

Don't blame your parents too much! We all had parents.

Katherine Mansfield

A picturesque child is charming, a sanitary one edifying, but a natural one is delightful.

Fanny Douglas

The tomboy element was conspicuous in me.

Lillie Langtry

When I was three, I used to run around the house, naked, singing. (I bet that comes as a shock!)

Cher

As a child I used to bite my toenails off instead of clipping them. I was very limber.

Julia Roberts

All those writers who write about their childhoods! Gentle God, if I wrote about mine you wouldn't sit in the same room with me.

Dorothy Parker

As a little girl, I always wanted to be heard, always knew what I was talking about – but nobody ever wanted to listen.

Mary J. Blige

Who would ever think that so much went on in the soul of a young girl?

Anne Frank

Children ask better questions than do adults.

Fran Lebowitz

Young people still have a remnant of sincerity.

Lady Mary Wortley Montagu

Family is set up to destroy the girl child's spirit.

Phyllis Chesler

I guess it was only within the security of my immediate family circle that I enjoyed that independent Theda Bara feeling.

Cornelia Otis Skinner

If I had a family motto, it would be Do What You Want, You Will Anyway.

Tama Janowitz

[My parents] had me absolutely convinced that I might not be able to have a hamburger in Woolworth's in Birmingham, but I could be president of the United States, if I wanted to be, and probably ought to be, from their point of view.

Condoleezza Rice

My sisters and I grew up in the great American tradition that decrees wealth, luxury and opportunity be counter-balanced by fear, unhappiness and repression.

Elaine Dundy

We were perfectly well treated but, up to a point, ignored. So we got on with our own lives and didn't expect much attention from the grown-ups. I don't think it did us any harm – rather the reverse. We observed the grown-ups a good deal more than they observed us.

Antonia White

Never imagine that children who don't say, or ask, don't know.

Rosamund Lehmann

51

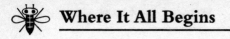

Where It All Begins

There are children of sane, functional families who turn out to be monstrous f***-ups, and children from what are considered textbook dysfunctional families that turn out OK.

Sophie Dahl

I am thankful to say that I never had an aunt who was afraid of seeming ridiculous.

Gwen Raverat

No grown-up … ever said sorry to a child in those days. None, in the event of inability to answer a question, ever confessed to simple ignorance. As for subjects such as birth, death, physical and sexual functions, these were taboo, and invested with an aura of murk, shame, guilt, suggestiveness and secrecy.

Rosamund Lehmann

One of the greatest happinesses of youth is the ignorance of evil.

Lady Mary Wortley Montagu

There is nothing in this world quite so wonderful as the faith a child has in one they love.

Calamity Jane

I really encourage my children to make mistakes. Make them as quickly and thoroughly as you can and go to the new step, because that's what life's about. What propel you to the next place are your mistakes, not your successes.

Susan Sarandon

The trouble about bringing up children is that it doesn't begin and end by making things nice for them.

Elizabeth Jane Howard

Youth gives a sense of new days dawning bright … But then youth is something which only exists in retrospect: you are barely conscious of it while you have it.

Fay Weldon

SCHOOLDAYS

If you educate a man you educate a person, but if you educate a woman you educate a family.

Ruby Manikan

The chief thing I learnt at school was how to tell lies.

Gwen Raverat

Stand firm in your refusal to remain conscious during algebra. In real life, I assure you, there is no such thing as algebra.

Fran Lebowitz

School was a bitch for me.

Cher

I was brought up in a very tough Catholic school. I was expelled for not smoking.

Rhonda Carling-Rodgers

I went to an all-girls school. That's why I ended up boy-mad.

Jenny Eclair

Thank goodness I was never sent to school; it would have rubbed off some of the originality.

Beatrix Potter

But then think how I was brought up! No school; mooning about alone among my father's books; never any chance to pick up all that goes on in schools – throwing balls; ragging: slang; vulgarity; scenes; jealousies …

Virginia Woolf

At nine I felt much pleasure from the effusions of my imaginations in the adorned drapery of versifications.

Elizabeth Barrett Browning

Good teaching is one-fourth preparation and three-fourths theatre.

Gail Godwin

The task of the educator lies in seeing that the child does not confound good with immobility and evil with activity.

Maria Montessori

I hated gym in high school. We had the standard-model gym teachers: paramilitary.

Fran Lebowitz

My class went to college in the era when you got a masters degrees in teaching because it was "something to fall back on" in the worst case scenario, the worst case scenario being that no one married you and you actually had to go to work.

Nora Ephron

I left school at fifteen having passed only one test – my cervical smear test.

Kathy Lette

A university education does little more than teach you how to spout second-hand opinions.

Shirley Conran

The purpose of "higher" education is not to educate but to exclude as many as possible from the various professions.

Valerie Solanas

In university they don't tell you that the greater part of the law is learning to tolerate fools.

Doris Lessing

BIRDS & BEES

I think when a boy is old enough to ask for a red-headed babysitter, he is old enough to stay home alone.

Ann Landers

When I was in school they showed us a sex education film about a boy calling up a girl on the phone and asking her out on a date. Nowadays I'm sure they show *9½ Weeks* or something starring Sharon Stone.

Ellen DeGeneres

Don't bother discussing sex with small children. They rarely have anything to add.

Fran Lebowitz

Sex is the tabasco sauce which an adolescent national palate sprinkles on every course in the menu.

Mary Day Winn

I remember once noticing, as an easily embarrassed teenager, that it felt strange to undress in front of an open book.

Shelley Jackson

Sex was not discussed in our house. Margaret Ann and I learned the difference between boys and girls the way most kids in our neighbourhood did. We took a friend's little brother down the cellar and made him take off his pants.

Patricia Neal

THE THRESHOLD OF MATURITY

When we tap into that girl part of us that usually got knocked out of us at about puberty, it's contacting a lot of power, a lot of humour, and a lot of solidarity.

Rebecca Wells

But society and popular culture are pretty much owned by extremely young people in so many ways. And their sensibility is not always the most evolved.

Lily Tomlin

The first compliment paid to a girl in her teens lingers longer in her memory than the subsequent pretty speeches that may be showered on her.

Lillie Langtry

Teenagers make anything look cool, including acne and self-pity.

Julie Burchill

Where It All Begins

The thing I find most depressing at the moment is how materialistic most of the students and young people I meet are ... People see the value of their future in terms of whether or not they'll have a Sony Walkman.

Rabbi Julia Neuberger

By the time I'd grown up, I naturally supposed that I'd grown up.

Eve Babitz

There is nothing can pay one for that invaluable ignorance which is the companion of youth, those sanguine groundless hopes, and that lively vanity which makes all the happiness of life.

Lady Mary Wortley Montagu

It is the prerogative of youth to be in a mess all the time.

Vicki Baum

My mom used to tell me to be glad I was different. She said, "Your day will come."

Cher

My mother always told me I wouldn't amount to anything because I procrastinate. I said, "Just wait."

Judy Tenuta

Your twenties are crap! They are exhausting. Because you're dancing for ten years. But I'm so tired, I want to go home. But I can't, I'm in my twenties. I've got to stay out and drink and take more drugs, and pretend I'm having fun with people I don't like. I just want to go home and read the Habitat catalogue.

Rhona Cameron

At this crossroads of your personality adventure read the sign, "Stop – Look – Missing!"

Renee Long

Love & How To Do It

DEFINITIONS OF LOVE

When people talk of glory, soul, or beauty, they are only talking of love.

Marie Bashkirtseff

I always feel the need for a feeling of worship in lovemaking, the feeling of something really sacred and close to you.

Alice Walker

Love makes one so receptive to everything beautiful.

Clara Schumann

To love deeply in one direction makes us more loving in all others.

Anne Sophie Swetchine

The head never rules the heart, but just becomes its partner in crime.

Mignon McLaughlin

Love has many keys besides that of her own dwelling.

Mary Cholmondeley

Love … does seem to have the faculty of taking your identity away from you and not always in the way the poets mention.

Mary McCarthy

♡ Love & How To Do It

Love is an exploding cigar which we willingly smoke.

Lynda Barry

Love is ... the remedy, the melody, the poison and the pain.

Louise Welsh

These are the things I know: you always throw spilled salt over your left shoulder, plant rosemary at your gate, keep lavender for luck and fall in love whenever possible.

Alice Hoffman

The potion drunk by lovers is prepared by no one but themselves.

Anaïs Nin

To fall in love you have to be in the state of mind for it to take, like a disease.

Nancy Mitford

We swoon with the thickness of our own tongue when we say, "I love you."

Djuna Barnes

Before I met my husband, I'd never fallen in love, though I'd stepped in it a few times.

Rita Rudner

We always think when we're in love that it is like nobody else's love, but I suspect we're more like everybody else at those times than at any other.

Elizabeth Jane Howard

The enthusiasm of a woman's love is even beyond the biographer's.

Jane Austen

If it is your time love will track you down like a cruise missile. If you say "No! I don't want it right now," that's when you'll get it for sure.

Lynda Barry

Love involves a peculiar unfathomable combination of understanding and misunderstanding.

Diane Arbus

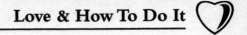

And remember that love is not leisure, it is work.

Anna Quindlen

Love is not to be bought … its silken wings are instantly shrivelled up when anything beside a return in kind is sought.

Mary Wollstonecraft

It requires much labour and a superior will to turn passion into a virtue. If we would raise the level of society, we must likewise raise the standard of our passions.

George Sand

Give until it hurts, because real love hurts.

Mother Teresa

THE PURSUIT OF LOVE

To be single after girlhood is a nuisance.

Ilka Chase

Volumes had been written about this creature, but they all treated the single girl like a scarlet-fever victim, a misfit … you can't really categorize one-third of the female population as misfits.

Helen Gurley Brown

And all the time in the background of our consciousness rings the warning that perhaps the right man will never come. A great love is given to very few.

Ruth Benedict

Single women in their thirties were saddled with an uneasy self-image: trapped somewhere between the Cosmo girl with own flat, own job, own car, having fun, and a Miss Havisham-style tragic barren spinster doomed to end up dying alone and being found three weeks later half-eaten by an alsatian.

Helen Fielding

All your life you wait around for some damn man!

Dorothy Parker

♡ Love & How To Do It

There are more women looking at men than there are stars looking at the earth.

Venetian proverb

Girls who collect men like postage stamps always get the wrong sort.

Sophie Tucker

Look at the rigid and formal race of old maids – the race whom all despise; they have fed themselves, from youth upwards, on maxims of resignation and endurance. Many of them get ossified with the dry diet.

Charlotte Brontë

We weren't meant to have futures, we were meant to marry them.

Nora Ephron

My mother was desperate to get me married. She used to say, "Sure he's a murderer. But he's a single murderer."

Joan Rivers

No matter how love-sick a woman is, she shouldn't take the first pill that comes along.

Joyce Brothers

I don't pop my cork for every guy I see.

Dorothy Fields

I'm really demanding. No girl really wants just a guy. You want a prince, you want Jesus. So when he comes around and his name is Steve, what are you supposed to do?

Macy Gray

Even in their early twenties most women are looking for a real man, not a middle-aged teenager wearing long pants and flashing their pay packet.

Mariella Frostrup

Give me a man that's human and careless and loves life, and one who can enjoy the rough-and-tumble of passion. I'd like to die spitting and swearing, you know, and I'm no mean wrestler!

Dorothy L. Sayers

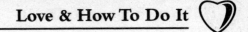

My advice to young women is to find a partner who has grown up with older sisters. They consider women important and they do not see them as an alien race. When you sit next to them, they talk to you.

Anne Robinson

I've had a few Mr Wrongs and I've been Mrs Wrong to some Mr Rights.

Kathy Burke

I don't have a boyfriend – it's tough when you're Serena Williams.

Serena Williams

I've discovered a lot of men are intimidated by success. I think, "I can't be less than I am so I'd need a man who is more."

Cilla Black

Of course I can get a man. Whenever I walk past a building site there are twenty guys shouting, "Doing anything on Tuesday, love?"

Minnie Driver

How did I meet Mick? You know, I always find that an offensive question. If you're intelligent and pretty you can meet anyone you want.

Bianca Jagger

Basically, Hugo was just like any other bloke you'd meet in a Greek myth.

Kathy Lette

The failure to find a marriageable man means the delicious prolongation of a late female adolescence: free and voluptuous, self-absorbed and female-centred.

Candace Bushnell

I'm a cheap date. You don't have to take me anywhere fancy.

Madonna

It's like being in a room with eight Labradors sniffing round you, and a Rottweiler who won't come near you – I know which one I'm drawn to.

Tara Palmer-Tomkinson

♥ Love & How To Do It

It is always inexpressibly difficult for me to believe that a man whom I like should be capable of not loving me.

Marie Bashkirtseff

When I am attracted to a man, I am like an Amazon in battle; I hit out in all directions.

Mae West

A man's ideal woman is the one he couldn't get.

Helen Rowland

Sex and the City is a show about female choice, not female rejection. All the straight men are crazy. If the gender roles were reversed, the producers would be accused by feminists of rank misogyny.

Candace Bushnell

Opportunity knocked. My doorman threw him out.

Adrienne E. Gusoff

When we attempt to buy love the price goes up, as with other commodities.

Ann Landers

Women who buy perfume and flowers for themselves because their men won't do it are called "self basting".

Adair Lara

Women who have many lovers are frequently those with a strong homely streak. They like a man in the house.

Ilka Chase

In actual fact, the female function is to relate, groove, love and be herself, irreplaceable by anyone else; the male function is to produce sperm. We now have sperm banks.

Valerie Solanas

I've been on so many blind dates, I should get a free dog.

Wendy Liebman

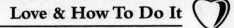
Lovers come in shoals or not at all.

Fay Weldon

LOVE RELATIONSHIPS

I know God has a plan for me, and it's not for me to live out my life by myself.

Jennifer Lopez

My life is a Rosary of Fierce Combats for Two, each bound together with the powerful magnetic chain of Sex.

Katherine Mansfield

What happens when you're a strong, complicated, questioning, vital person? There aren't many guys who aren't threatened by that. So you learn as a woman to sit on little aspects of yourself, or sugar-coat it. You minimize yourself constantly.

Susan Sarandon

If you wish to live with a man in harmony while you can, there is no other way but play-acting. Then, every now and then, to your fearful consternation, the play-acting will come alive, and you will be no longer play-acting. But it is essential that he cannot detect which is which.

Caitlin Thomas

In the love affair, as in sculpture, poetry, and every other fine art, no lasting success can be achieved without skill.

Doris Langley Moore

A woman cannot be wholly natural with a man – there is always a feeling that she must take care that she doesn't let him go.

Katherine Mansfield

The woman says, "I never know if you love me, Jonathan," and the man replies smoothly, "Well, I'm here, aren't I?"

Lynne Truss

I crave nothing but constant love and attention.

Fay Weldon

♡ Love & How To Do It

Each coming together of man and wife, even if they have been mated for many years, should be a fresh adventure; each winning should necessitate a fresh wooing.

Marie Stopes

You fall in love with somebody for big reasons, but they manifest themselves in the small things, and pretty soon you can't tell if you love the quirks because they're his, or you love him because of the quirks.

Hazel McClay

Only one who understands the architecture of the love affair can build the superior structure which houses love itself.

Doris Langley Moore

I like the word affection, because it signifies something habitual.

Mary Wollstonecraft

When you move in house with someone, and you're carrying all that heavy stuff, your stereo, your books, your CDs, that's when you should say: "By the way, could you help me in with my rather heavy emotional baggage as well? Here's the first suitcase, that's insecurity, jealousy, possessiveness."

Rhona Cameron

Two people calling each other darlings, angels, and ducks cannot last.

Harriette Wilson

It's a pity to be friends with a lover. It's giving him a second part of yourself.

Brigitte Bardot

Love has nothing to do with living together – on the contrary, most of the time it dies from it.

Colette

A different taste in jokes is a great strain on the affections.

George Eliot

Any love, when it's mistreated, deteriorates.

Jennifer Lopez

A spark between two people can lead to a short circuit.

Amanda Marteleur

You know that when I hate you, it is because I love you to a point of passion that unhinges my soul.

Julie Lespinasse

Maybe the quest for equality in a relationship as the ideal is misleading. Perhaps we should be looking for a sort of interesting seesaw.

Zoë Heller

Love never dies of starvation, but often of indigestion.

Ninon de Lenclos

I despise a man who gives in to me.

Edith Templeton

People live out relationships so differently that it's dangerous to make judgements. A relationship might seem full of conflict, but that's their default setting.

Reverend Dianna Gwilliams

It is not a sin to be incompatible.

Anna Pasternak

I think we all have the capacity to really love without expectation, but that's really evolved, isn't it? I mean, I'm up for receiving, really.

Annie Lennox

Once a woman has forgiven her man, she must not reheat his sins for breakfast.

Marlene Dietrich

There is a charm in the humility of a lover who has offended. The charm is so great that we like to prolong it.

Harriette Wilson

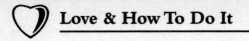 **Love & How To Do It**

It is easier to keep half a dozen lovers guessing than to keep one lover after he has stopped guessing.

Helen Rowland

Nothing, I think, can be more wanting in dignity than a woman's continuing to persecute a man who is evidently tired of her.

Lady Trelawney in Lady Caroline Lamb's Glenarvon

Sexual Desire & Gratification

SEX

If we weren't meant to have sex, He wouldn't have given us the dangly bits that get us turned on.

Edwina Currie

Unless you've got a bit of earth, mud and sex in you, there's no heart really.

Dawn French

"Six inches of snow on twenty feet of lava" had been said of me, and not without reason.

Marie d'Agoult

Sex and I have a lot in common. I don't want to take any credit for inventing it – but I may say, in my own modest way, and in a manner of speaking – that I have rediscovered it!

Mae West

Touch is the oldest sense, and the most urgent.

Diane Ackerman

The power of one sex over the other does certainly begin sooner, and end later than one should think.

Hester Thrale

Sex is the refuge of the mindless.

Valerie Solanas

67

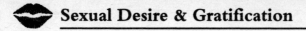

Passionate sex is not about intimacy but about something more raw, shocking, forbidden.

Hazel McClay

There is an etiquette, a protocol, even in impetuous, runaway sex.

Diane Ackerman

In the hands of Nature, sex is a tyrant's weapon.

Stevie Smith

SEX EDUCATION

I prayed it was all some sick joke mothers were forced to tell their daughters.

Rosie O'Donnell

When I was in high school in the early sixties, nice girls didn't go all the way – most of us wouldn't have known how to. But man, could we kiss!

Diane Ackerman

A kiss can be a comma, a question mark, or an exclamation point. That's the basic spelling that every woman ought to know.

Mistinguette

They used to say that if you lost your virginity in Cork (Ireland) someone would be sure to find it before teatime and bring it back to your mother.

Maeve Binchy

Royal tradition demands that only a virgin is fit for marriage to the future king – and look where that got everybody.

Kate Spicer

The young always think that they invented sex and somehow hold full literary rights on the subject.

Mary Wesley

My parents were so resolutely chaste I assumed they must have bought me from a shop rather than indulging in the unsavoury business of conception.

Wendy Perriam

Popular culture talked ad nauseam about love, love, love, but gave us virtually no useful information at all about it. It didn't seem fair.

Nancy Wartik

Tony Randall and I were once doing a variety show together, and the first thing he said to me was something about fellatio. I don't think I'd ever heard that word before, and I said, "I haven't read much Shakespeare."

Janeane Garofalo

If sex is so personal, why are we expected to share it with someone else?

Lily Tomlin

When men discover a girl hasn't been with anybody else, they react in one of three ways. They either want to take you home to meet their mother before marrying you; or they want to plant their flag where no one else has been; or they pat you on the head like a little sister and become all protective and brotherly.

Lulu

I've always persuaded the man I was in love with that he had to teach me everything, even when I could have taught him a thing or two.

Barbara Cartland

When mom found my diaphragm, I told her it was a bathing cap for my cat.

Liz Winston

If sex is such a natural phenomenon, how come there are so many books on how to?

Bette Midler

CAN'T GET NO SATISFACTION

The soap-operas do us a tremendous disservice, because they show us different sexual experiences every single episode, with a highness of emotion and satisfaction, and nobody in real life can duplicate that.

Ruth Westheimer

My heart demands more excitement than anyone can give it. My frail body is exhausted by the act of love. Never is it the love I dream of.

Sarah Bernhardt

Women should feel like having sex is giving something back to them, replenishing them, not taking the last microbe of energy they have.

Susie Bright

Our sex life was a disgrace to sex.

Rosamund Lehmann

After we made love he took a piece of chalk and made an outline of my body.

Joan Rivers

Much more genius is needed to make love than to command armies.

Ninon de Lenclos

For years I went to bed with men because I wanted their affection, which is what I thought the exchange involved.

Elizabeth Jane Howard

It is remarkable how much some men think they are entitled to in exchange for dinner and an evening at the theatre.

Ilka Chase

Baby talk is not an aphrodisiac.

Cynthia Heimel

For females, word-play is foreplay. But for blokes?

Kathy Lette

Grab the penis, it breaks the ice, it's kind of a fun friendly thing to do!

Cynthia Heimel

Just remember what you have learned in the sexual technique book you read: foreplay, foreplay, foreplay … in the right location, location, location.

"Mom", the agony aunt for the tartcity website

Shopping is better than sex. At least if you're not satisfied, you can exchange it for something you really like.

Adrienne E. Gusoff

Men make love more intensely at twenty, but make love better, however, at thirty.

Catherine the Great

Real gratification is not enshrined in a tiny cluster of nerves but in the sexual involvement of the whole person.

Germaine Greer

And whenever does anybody come together? The whole history of sex is a disgraceful pigsty of mistiming.

Caitlin Thomas

The female orgasm is more of a mystery than the continued career success of George W. Bush.

Kathy Lette

It is okay if you have a small penis. But, realistically speaking, it is not okay to have a small penis and also be lousy in bed.

"Mom", the agony aunt for the tartcity website

Most men would probably prefer to swallow the postcoital cigarette than hear an honest answer to: "Was that good for you?"

Barbara Ellen

The fact that good people and bad people have orgasms should tell you God has a sense of irony.

Susan Sarandon

TOO MUCH OF A GOOD THING ...

Our bed's only MFI; it won't take multiple orgasm.

Victoria Wood

When it comes to sexuality, hypocrisy has long been America's middle name.

Naomi Wolf

Single acts of intercourse can topple governments.

Fay Weldon

Things are different now people (at least pretend to) have an enormous amount of sex and tell everybody else about it.

Tilda Swinton

Sex should neither be seen nor heard. Certainly not talked about afterwards.

Caitlin Thomas

You don't have to have sex to be in love. I've never had sex. I don't think I will ever have sex. I think that's what keeps me going. I hear it's good fun, though. I think it's much sexier to have not had sex.

Stella McCartney

I seem to be the first person in history who doesn't think about sex from one week to the next. Romans, Vikings and Visigoths thought about sex all day.

Lucy Ellman

People who got too intense about sex were a little outré. It was like wearing plastic spikes with rhinestones and meaning it, it was like taking mink coats seriously.

Margaret Atwood

What is it about marriage that makes it a kind of metaphorical cold shower for everyone involved?

Susan Maushart

Marriage and macaroni – if they are not hot, they are not good.

Venetian proverb

Women who spent most of their single lives running after sex often find that they spend a good deal of their married life trying hard to avoid it.

Susan Maushart

Many wives will feel great sympathy for the widow discovered sleeping beside the corpse of her husband, three years after he died. How is a woman to guess something's up – especially when the conversation and the sex are as good as they've ever been?

Carol Sarler

I think I've done my quota.

Diane von Furstenberg

A marriage without sex is what I call friendship.

Mariella Frostrup

INDECOROUS ACTS

Sex is a bad thing because it rumples the clothes.

Jackie Onassis

Whatever else can be said about sex, it cannot be called a dignified performance.

Helen Lawrenson

I could never be comfortable at an orgy. I'd always think there would be someone making rabbit ears behind my back.

Diane Nichols

I've had the piano redesigned: all Tommy's tattoos are now carved on it. There's a swing above it, like a fairy tale. Tommy likes me to have a swing before dinner. He sits there, playing away, while I take off my clothes and swing naked above him.

Pamela Anderson

You know the worst thing about oral sex? The view.

Maureen Lipman

Of course, it was all based on sex, darling, like most things in life. Did you know she was a nut-cracker? It was a trick she learned in a brothel in Shanghai. He, poor love, had never enjoyed proper sex before, and she soon had him totally enslaved.

Barbara Cartland on the relationship between Edward VIII and Wallis Simpson

Fondling a man's privates is not like testing peaches in the supermarket.

Cynthia Heimel

Don't criticize in the sack. Discuss constructively later.

Ruth Westheimer

When the grandmothers of today hear the word "Chippendales", they don't necessarily think of chairs.

Jean Kerr

I never quite know what people mean when they brag about how they are like animals in bed. Which animal? A big scary tiger? A gerbil?

Barbara Ellen

True Romance

TRUE ROMANCE IS DEAD

The historical Saint Valentine was clubbed to death, you know.

Lynne Truss

Love's a thin diet, nor will keep out cold.

Aphra Behn

Only hopeless romantics need to be told yet again that love is an illusion, that it dies, that it is for lunatics, addicts and fools. The rest of us may occasionally like – even love – a little respite from what we know.

Lorrie Moore

Everyone says that women are in control of these things, and, yes, to a certain extent we are, but it is still viewed as emasculating to set out your requirements at the off: dinner, 8.30pm-10.30pm; unbridled passion, 10.30pm-11.30pm; postcoital chitchat, 11.30pm-11.35pm; embarrassed silence, 11.35pm-11.55pm; carriages at midnight.

Maria McErlane

THE REAL THING

There's no substitute for moonlight and kissing.

Barbara Cartland

A young woman in love is a titanic force.

Lorrie Moore

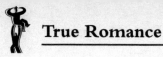# True Romance

Durable love is a diamond requiring a case of pure gold, and your soul is that precious tabernacle.

George Sand

Real love comes calling on the wings of respect.

Mariella Frostrup

Juliet, dagger plunged into chest, was pure machismo compared to Romeo and his delicate, mishandled poison drinking.

Lorrie Moore

My notion of love was not unlike the blue rose: simple and impossible.

Hazel McClay

We don't believe in rheumatism and true love until after the first attack.

Marie von Ebner Eschenbach

If love can bear everything, then love can even more easily replace everything.

Marie d'Agoult

INFATUATIONS

Falling in love consists merely in uncorking the imagination and bottling the common-sense.

Helen Rowland

In love, lovelorn, anything having to do with romantic love, has nothing to do with the ostensible ability to think.

Fran Lebowitz

We do fall in love when we're young and we idolize images, thoughts and ideas instead of real things.

Goldie Hawn

It is said there is no happiness, and no love to be compared to that which is felt for the first time. Most persons erroneously think so; but love like other arts requires experience.

Lady Caroline Lamb

Misunderstanding keepeth Love alive.

Katherine Mansfield

The mark of a true crush (whether the object is a man, woman or city) is that you fall in love first and grope for reasons afterward.

Shana Alexander

I married the first man I ever kissed. When I tell my children that they just about throw up.

Barbara Bush

Infatuation doesn't look for superior qualities in its object, or else detects such qualities in the silliest irrelevancies but, God, what those silly details do to your metabolism!

Vicki Baum

Of course, unconditional love is a mirage.

Anne Karpf

THE MARRIAGE VOWS

Let's be honest – a wedding is absolutely the worst way to start married life.

Caitlin Moran

If the bridegroom does not show up, marry the best man. After a few weeks you will not be able to notice the difference between them.

Helen Rowland

Marriage is what happens when one at least of the partners doesn't want the other to get away.

Fay Weldon

The average man looks on matrimony as a hitching post where he can tie a woman and leave her until he comes home nights.

Helen Rowland

It was a mixed marriage. I'm human, he was a Klingon.

Carol Leifer

The "vicious circle" in a bachelor's opinion, is the platinum one on a woman's third finger.

Helen Rowland

If we all were alike honourable and true, as I wish to be, it would be unnecessary to bind men and women together by law, since two persons who may have chosen each other from affection, possessing heart and honour, could not part.

Harriette Wilson

I have given the art and practice of marriage much thought ... I think it demands the capacity to endure, surmount, cope with, fight for a shared and continuous intimacy, and that is something few people can accept.

M. F. K. Fisher

And I have learned a long time ago that the only people who count in any marriage are the two that are in it.

Hillary Rodham Clinton

Verily, my daughter, a husband is a good thing. He giveth a house a "finished look", even as a rubber plant and a door-plate.

Helen Rowland

The divine right of husbands, like the divine right of kings, may, it is hoped, in this enlightened age, be contested without danger.

Mary Wollstonecraft

The more I think of marriage, the further removed from it I feel! It is an institution that ought to be confined to temperamental old maids, weary prostitutes, and royalties!

Violet Keppel

You get a hundred dollars a week for filing, and a hundred dollars a night for fucking, but you don't get nuthin' for filing, and fucking, and cleaning, and cooking, and washing, and ironing, and chauffeuring, and nursing ...

Florynce Kennedy

True Romance

My God, who wouldn't want a wife?

Judy Syfers

I married in part because I knew no better way to disconnect from my first family. I wanted what I saw as a full woman's life, whatever was possible.

Adrienne Rich

The exterior architecture of the contemporary marriage emphasizes fluidity, simplicity and light. No wonder it's got such fantastic street appeal. Venture inside, however, and you're in for a nasty shock.

Susan Maushart

"The wife before marriage," say I, "is Pompeii before the eruption; and the wife after marriage is Pompeii after the eruption."

Marie Bashkirtseff

I'm more afraid of marriage than of death.

Shakira

Given that marriage increases a man's life expectancy and decreases a woman's, logically we should be the ones to offer it. It's our sacrifice, after all.

Victoria Coren

I don't know that I could have handled work, children, and husband. Work and children I could have. But the husband was too much.

Diane von Furstenberg

When you're young, you think of marriage as a train you simply have to catch. You run and run until you've caught it, and then you sit back and look out of the window and realize you're bored.

Elizabeth Bowen

I never wanted to get married. I felt it was just a bad contract to get into.

Deborah Harry

True Romance

Being married is not the problem. Nor is being a parent, or at least not in the same way. The problem is being a wife.

Susan Maushart

Having a wife and children must be seen by men for the enormous privilege that it is: the pearl of great price for which no sacrifice is too great.

Susan Maushart

Self-sacrifice is the leit-motif of most of the marital games played by women, from the crudest ("I've given you the best years of my life") to the most sophisticated ("I only went to bed with him so's he'd promote you").

Germaine Greer

Those men who lead a gay life in their youth, and arrive at middle age with feelings blunted and passions exhausted, who have but one aim in marriage, the selfish advancement of their interest, and to think that such men take as wives, as second selves, women young, modest, sincere, pure in heart and life, with feeling all fresh, and emotions all unworn, and bind such virtue and vitality to their own withered existence, such sincerity to their own hollowness, such disinterestedness to their own haggard avarice – to think this – troubles the soul to its inmost depths.

Charlotte Brontë

Ideally, couples need three lives; one for him, one for her, and one for them together.

Jacqueline Bisset

It is absurd to suggest that a wife should be on 24-hour call like an inhalator squad – ready for romance at the drop of a hint.

Ann Landers

Of course people can't carry their party manners into marriage; but if they could, marriage would be more like a party and less like a prize fight.

Helen Rowland

True Romance

Few husbands realize what a tenuous hold they have on their wives. Like magnets, they only attract within a limited range.

Elizabeth Forsythe Hailey

What woman doesn't think when she looks at her man dressed in his boxer shorts picking his toenails in front of the Mets game, "This is the guy I decide to end the quest for?"

Jill Bialovsky

Wasn't there a day in your life when, faithful, loving, even in love, you suddenly looked at him and shrank back in astonishment: "What is this man doing in my house with me?"

Colette

It might help you to be more satisfied with your mate if you remember that when you made the selection it was not multiple choice.

Phyllis Diller

Marriage is supposed to be an immunization against loneliness.

Kathy Lette

Marriage is the only thing that affords a woman the pleasure of company and the perfect sensation of solitude at the same time.

Helen Rowland

Marriage is not friendship.

Fanny Kemble

Indeed, for females, depression and marriage go together like the proverbial horse and carriage.

Susan Maushart

We've just marked our tenth wedding anniversary on the calendar and threw darts at it.

Phyllis Diller

Marriage has a funny dynamic. All of a sudden things change, and you expect something different from the person you married. All this stuff comes into play, and it is not simply about loving someone. Things have to come into sync, you have to be on the same page.

Jennifer Lopez

I do not ever allow my husband to think that he fully knows me, that he has that access.

Cynthia Kling

Never depend on immersion in another person for your personal growth: for the creation of your real personality: for the other person is merely preying on you to create their own. As you are preying on them …

Caitlin Thomas

It's easier to criticize marriage when you're married; you sound wisely disillusioned rather than simply bitter.

Daphne Merkin

Women stick like glue to their men. It's as if once partnered we are imprinted, so that it takes the emotional equivalent of a surgical procedure to remove us.

Margaret Cook

Historically, marrying for passion is a relatively new phenomenon – one that just happens to correspond with the rising divorce rate.

Hazel McClay

The couple who "tell the truth to each other" after their first visit to the marriage-guidance counsellor seldom enjoy many more nights together.

Fay Weldon

BROKEN HEARTS

Women cannot walk out of the traps of love, but men can; they have wars and revolutions to attend to.

Anaïs Nin

True Romance

Love is both healer and the warrior that sends the arrows to their mark.

Stephanie June Sorréll

You don't die of a broken heart, you only wish you did.

Marilyn Peterson

The hunger of love is much more difficult to remove than the hunger for bread.

Mother Teresa

Falling out of love is very enlightening. For a short while you see the world with new eyes.

Iris Murdoch

Allowances should be made for the newly separated, particularly the women, who ask you round for drinks because they can't stand the loneliness and then cancel at the last moment because they can't face the togetherness. They also tend to ring you on Boxing Day, saying that they might drop in, so you stay in all day. They never turn up. Later you find that they have done the same to six other people.

Jilly Cooper

The sorrows of a mistress when losing the lover she adores, has been the theme of every age. Poetry and painting, have exhausted the expression of her despair.

Lady Caroline Lamb

The only relationships I haven't wrecked right away were the ones that wrecked me later.

Jane Rosenthal in Melissa Bank's The Girls' Guide to Hunting and Fishing

I hope I don't fall in love again. It's so terrible to fall in love.

Yoko Ono

Nothing easier than to make fun of a love when it's past. It would be nice and spare us a lot of despair if one could apply the same humorous detachment to a love that's still present and alive.

Vicki Baum

True Romance

Breaking my heart will not do, 'tis like breaking a looking glass – the figure still lives in every broken piece, and will continue till annihilation.

Hester Thrale

I don't regret any of the relationships I've had, even the ones that practically killed me.

Susan Sarandon

Once it's off, it's off. There's nothing more dead than dead love.

Tara Palmer-Tomkinson

Now my barrier's always up, I'm not getting hurt for no one, not again. I fall in love well easy, but I don't show it.

Jordan

I picked up the pieces and my credit card and shopped back my womanly dignity.

Kerry Herlihy

I am no longer afraid of being on my own. Nor am I scared of having my heart broken. There are so many arrows coming at us all the time that it never happens the same way twice.

Lulu

DIVORCE

You have left a marriage long before you actually pick up your bags and walk out.

Anna Pasternak

Divorce typically lowers a woman's standard of living by seventy-three per cent and raises a man's by forty-two per cent – but emotionally.

Susan Maushart

It's true that some couples have "arrangements". Usually, the husband arranges to have sex with other women, and the wife arranges to divorce him.

Barbara Ellen

I don't believe in divorce. I believe in widowhood.

Carolyn Green

Changing husbands is only changing troubles.

Kathleen Norris

A woman voting for divorce is like a turkey voting for Christmas.

Alice Glynn

One of the terrors of divorce is the knowledge that the safe place, home, has become a source of danger and betrayal: and there is nowhere, psychically or physically, to which to return.

Fay Weldon

People talk a lot about the high rates of divorce but at the turn of the twentieth century life expectancy for women was only forty-five, so a lot of divorces now would have been deaths in previous centuries.

Dorothy Rowe

Divorced women seem to be a dime a dozen, while divorced men get treated like precious commodities.

Daphne Merkin

No divorcees were included, except those who had shown signs of penitence by being remarried to the very wealthy.

Edith Wharton

It Takes A Good Girl
To Be Bad

JEALOUSY & INFIDELITY

Jealousy is the lifelong noose hanging about the neck of love.

Caitlin Thomas

Women who are possessive are embarrassing and evil.

Ilka Chase

What makes me jealous? The slightest shift in attention.

Fran Lebowitz

Love, from its very nature, must be transitory. To seek for a secret that would render it constant, would be as wild a search as for the philosopher's stone, or the grand panacea: and the discovery would be equally useless, or rather pernicious, to mankind.

Mary Wollstonecraft

What do you want? Forever Amber?

Tallulah Bankhead

It is not possible to have only one man. Deep in my heart, I change.

Brigitte Bardot

I'm also turning into a bit of a commitment phobic myself, a bit of a man, a bloke.

Tara Palmer-Tomkinson

It Takes A Good Girl To Be Bad

If you're looking for monogamy, you'd better marry a swan.

Nora Ephron

A hard dog to keep on the porch.

Hillary Rodham Clinton on her husband, Bill

It is better to be unfaithful than to be faithful without wanting to be.

Brigitte Bardot

Never try to make a husband your husband.

Kerry Herlihy

You mean apart from my own?

Zsa Zsa Gabor, when asked how many husbands she'd had

Infidelity for the unattached party is like dinner with no food: an empty invitation.

Mariella Frostrup

Never take him seriously when he complains about his wife.

Kerry Herlihy

The wife is about striving for some notion of perfection. The mistress is about games, invention, closeness.

Cynthia Kling

Whenever I hear about a love triangle or ménage à trois, my first thought is that somebody is going to come out a loser.

Daphne Merkin

I'm sure he'll find someone else to be unfaithful to soon.

Jerry Hall on Mick Jagger

If men couldn't trade in their wives for twenty-year-old women, they wouldn't.

Tama Janowitz

If all those men are having affairs then, unless I'm wrong, they must be having them with us women. Therefore, we're probably having as many affairs as men.

Lucy Cavendish

It Takes A Good Girl To Be Bad

More divorces start in the bedroom than in any other room of the house.

Ann Landers

If my vagina could monologue it would have only one thing to say: you lying, cheating, hypocritical bastard.

Kathy Lette

The best thing I have is the knife from *Fatal Attraction*. I hung it in my kitchen. It's my way of saying, Don't mess with me.

Glenn Close

Don't think you count as the one and only wife, till you see who turns up at the crematorium, tearful over your old man.

Fay Weldon

How do people have affairs these days? How on earth do they manage it? You know, with itemized phone bills and call back, and email and CCTV everywhere. I suppose people find a way.

Joan Bakewell

You do sort of forgive what some might consider unforgivable.

Hillary Rodham Clinton

PROMISCUITY OR PRISSINESS

Everything in life is like being a whore, isn't it? All give and take.

Xaviera Hollander

Your morals are like roads through the Alps. They make these hairpin turns all the time.

Erica Jong

Never, ever go to bed with a man on the first date. Not ever. Unless you really want to.

Cynthia Heimel

Slut is a style statement, honey.

Kate Spicer

It Takes A Good Girl To Be Bad

Look at the parts the Oscar-nominated actresses played this year: hooker, hooker, hooker, hooker, and nun.

Nora Ephron

Tart. It's a potent four-letter word. Sweet, sour, sharp, sexy, bad, with a touch of cheesecake.

Stella Duffy

I've always felt that prostitutes are in control of the streets, not victims.

Camille Paglia

When I'm good I'm very good, but when I'm bad I'm better.

Mae West

I think [AIDS has] caused a return to false values – i.e. the right wing, the fundamentalists – where "If you're a good person to begin with, this wouldn't be happening".

Sandra Bernhard

When I was a girl it was drilled into us that whoever crossed her legs was no lady. Try sitting for an hour or more without crossing your legs and you'd just as soon be a hussy.

Cornelia Otis Skinner

It Takes A Good Girl To Be Bad.

Sophie Tucker

The soul of me goes into the streets and craves love of the casual stranger, begs and prays for a little of the precious poison.

Katherine Mansfield

Your average woman has been round the block so many times she has worn a groove.

Kate Spicer

I'm certain I was a prostitute in some other life.

Shirley MacLaine

A man can sleep around, no questions asked, but if a woman makes nineteen or twenty mistakes she's a tramp.

Joan Rivers

It Takes A Good Girl To Be Bad

I don't mind tarts, and I don't mind ladies, much, if they are bona-fide, but I can't stand the socially impeccable darlings with the cheap little souls, masquerading as moral virgins and pulling tricks an honest whore would blush at.

Ilka Chase

The only difference between a gold-digger and a sex worker is that one of them admits to trading sex for money.

Tracey Cox

If you are sleeping around to get experience for Mr Right, you can stop now. Mr Right will not view your list of bed-partners as impressive credentials.

Ann Landers

There is no such thing as casual sex. Only emotionally careless sex.

Mariella Frostrup

Love is like playing checkers. You have to know which man to move.

Jackie 'Moms' Mabley

When the sun comes up, I have morals again.

Elayne Boosler

Promiscuity is boring, much more than fish and chips, which is comforting.

Edna O'Brien

New-style women's mags may talk the language of Loaded, but how many women really walk the walk?

Lisa Hilton

Friendship & Isolation

THE NATURE OF FRIENDSHIP

Friendship I say is the vine-prop of life.

Virginia Woolf

By friendship, I mean an entire communication of thoughts, wishes, interests, and pleasures, being undivided; a mutual esteem, which naturally carries with it a pleasing sweetness of conversation, and terminates in the desire of making one or another happy.

Lady Mary Wortley Montagu

A good friend beats a bad lover any day.

Mariella Frostrup

Don't you have to be hospitalized with hilarity on girls' nights out?

Kathy Lette

I am a good friend to my friends … Without them I would have nothing of interest to say to anyone, because I would be a cardboard cut-out.

Anna Quindlen

I have been blessed with heroic friendships.

Isak Dinesen

Women's friendships are unspoken and undervalued.

Anita Diamant

Crowd females together, in convent, hospital or school, and they fall into psychic step and menstruate together, in tune with the phases of the moon.

Fay Weldon

My girlfriends are usually making "Who lit the fuse on *your* tampon?" taunts by now.

Kathy Lette

We were so terrific together. Her so tall with all that hair. Me so tall with no hair.

Grace Jones on her party days with Jerry Hall

A lot of warm vulgarity is incomparably preferable to a little bit of pinched niceness.

Caitlin Thomas

Friendship to me is like a capital reserve. It pays dividends only so long as the principal remains intact.

Elizabeth Forsythe Hailey

I look for loyalty in my friends. That and returning phone calls.

Diane Modahl

It's men who find deep friendships between women strangest. For them the intimacy signals possession, treachery, *trouble*.

Maureen Freely

In some cultures, women are regarded as the sieves through whom the best-guarded secrets will sift.

Margaret Mead

FRIENDS IN NEED

People are friends because they're going to get something out of it. The friend you can call at two in the morning – that's getting something.

Tama Janowitz

Friendship & Isolation

Everyone wants to ride with you in the limo, but what you need is someone who will take the bus with you when the limo breaks down.

Oprah Winfrey

A friend in need is a right pain in the arse.

Jenny Eclair

Man is made for sympathy. It is the deepest want and the highest privilege of his nature.

Harriet Martineau

Nothing kills a female friendship faster than an admission of fear, failure, misery or confusion that isn't immediately reciprocated.

Maureen Freely

Sometimes I think that it is the sole purpose of girlfriends to give false hope.

Jane Slavin

A friend will … threaten to kill anyone who tries to come into a room where you are trying on bathing suits.

Erma Bombeck

You fall in love, you may just as well issue a statement to your friends: "Bye, see you in five years. When we've broken up. And we really need you."

Rhona Cameron

The best time to make friends is before you need them.

Ethel Barrymore

BREAKDOWN OF FRIENDSHIP

When I take a liking to a person I must and will be something to them; so if they will not like me I always make it my business and peculiar care that they shall dislike and quarrel with me. Let me once get them into a quarrel and I am sure of them.

Harriette Wilson

It is little *unspoken-of* grievances rankling in the mind that weaken affection.

Elizabeth Gaskell

I've had relationships that I thought ran deep that ultimately were over the next day. I'm not talking about men, but girlfriends.

Tama Janowitz

Hell hath no fury like a best friend scorned.

Barbara Ellen

If it's very painful for you to criticize your friends – you're safe in doing it. But if you take the slightest pleasure in it, that's the time to hold your tongue.

Alice Duer Miller

ISOLATION

I think I was born lonely. It's the accompaniment I've always known.

Annie Lennox

The heart may think it knows better: the senses know that absence blots people out. We have really no absent friends.

Elizabeth Bowen

Winter & lack of friends are dreadful evils.

Mary Shelley

I've never belonged to any group or huddle of any kind. You cannot be an artist and work collectively.

Katherine Anne Porter

I love my friends tenderly and blindly. All others I have profoundly detested. I feel no ardour now for hatred; but I am cold as death to those whom I do not know.

George Sand

My two greatest needs and desires – smoking cigarettes and plotting revenge – are basically solitary pursuits.

Fran Lebowitz

Friendship & Isolation

My life is what I expected it to be – sometimes when I wake in the morning – and know that Solitude, Remembrance and Longing are to be almost my sole companions all day through – that at night I shall go to bed with them, that they will long keep me sleepless – that next morning I shall wake to them again –

Charlotte Brontë

When I am happy I seek my friends – when harassed & uncomfortable I shut myself up in my shell.

Mary Shelley

Living in a vacuum sucks.

Adrienne E. Gusoff

Dreams have only one owner at a time. That's why dreamers are lonely.

Erma Bombeck

Sometimes, after a delightful evening spent with perfect hosts in a full, groaning family house, a single person spends the next few days dumb with misery.

Lynne Truss

I have an absolute antipathy towards shy people to this day, because I think it's lazy and dull.

Jenny Eclair

We find lonely people who are known only by their addresses, by the number of their room. Where are we, then? Do we really know that there are such people? These are the people we must know.

Mother Teresa

And then, of course, if one's lonely, one often feels rather superior too.

Stevie Smith

Gods & Goddesses:
Religions & Creeds

FAITH

Make one home for thyself, my daughter. One actual home … and another spiritual home, which thou art to carry with thee always.

Catherine of Siena

Nobody can deny but religion is a comfort to the distressed, a cordial to the sick, and sometimes a restraint on the wicked; therefore whoever would argue or laugh it out of the world without giving some equivalent for it ought to be treated as a common enemy.

Lady Mary Wortley Montagu

When I look back on the fantastic mess of my life, my one hope is that God can make something of it.

Antonia White

In India there is great respect for holiness, even among rascals.

Mother Teresa

Loving or feeble natures need a positive religion, a visible refuge, a protection …

Margaret Fuller

God has come down so low, I mean so far from Himself, in order to look for me.

Liane de Pougy

✳ Gods & Goddesses

No one can live without that constant sense of the divine within one.

Sonja Tolstoy

All my religion is from my heart, and not from books.

Harriette Wilson

Comprehending your deity and being in harmony with his plan is to be saved.

Jane Addams

I know God will not give me anything I can't handle. I just wish that He didn't trust me so much.

Mother Teresa

I believe, unlike you, that God is not floating in the ether, but unbudgeably lodged, in differing sizes, in the heads of every single person on the earth. And he grows and responds in exact measure to the amount of work we do for him.

Caitlin Thomas

Piety teaches resignation … The better I am acquainted with it, the more charms I find.

Theodosia Burr

God says very clearly: "Even if a mother could forget her child – I will not forget you – I have carved you in the palm of my hand."

Mother Teresa

The soul has not got to live permanently under a stone, like a bloated beetle in the dark. That is the Christian method of keeping uppish people down.

Caitlin Thomas

Religion should not be sophisticated; when it is, it loses all humanity.

Anita Loos

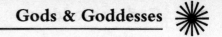

Most Englishmen, if forced into analyzing their own creeds –
which Heaven forbid – are convinced that God is an Englishman,
probably educated at Eton.

E. M. Delafield

You can safely assume that you've created God in your own image
when it turns out that God hates all the same people you do.

Anne Lamott

I read the book of Job last night – I don't think God comes out
well in it.

Virginia Woolf

Christianity always annoys me. I think all that emphasis on the
Cross is defeatist.

Barbara Cartland

I often have a suspicion God is still trying to work things out and
hasn't finished.

Rebecca West

When I found out I thought God was white, and a man, I lost
interest.

Celie in Alice Walker's The Colour Purple

Men don't get cellulite. God might just be a man.

Rita Rudner

THE VIRGIN MARY

If I were going to convert to any religion I would probably choose
Catholicism because it at least has female saints and the Virgin
Mary.

Margaret Atwood

I was fired from [the convent], finally, for a lot of things, among
them my insistence that the Immaculate Conception was
spontaneous combustion.

Dorothy Parker

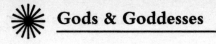

Gods & Goddesses

We feminists are supposed to have a problem with Mary – the pristine, perfect image of womanhood who makes the rest of us look like sin-drenched slappers.

Julie Burchill

Personally I blame the Virgin Mary. She was too passive! If only she had been more assertive ... turned round to God and said: "No! Piss off ... I'm sorry but I'm not that kind of virgin! ... I'm saving myself for Buddha."

Rhonda Carling-Rodgers

PRAYING

At my first communion I was not seeking anything at all, in those days I was a heedless, greedy little beast, a hot-blooded young animal chafing at the bit, laughing at Hell, pausing at neither the Passion nor the Cross.

Liane de Pougy

My mother went to church because she thought that if she didn't, a great weight would fall from the sky and kill her.

Julie Walters

I say my prayers in my diary because I usually fall asleep if I say my prayers out loud.

Britney Spears

Prayer became synonymous for me with giving up hope; if ever I prayed again, it was only in a final frenzy of despair, and was the first step towards resignation at not getting what I wanted.

Gwen Raverat

ALTERNATIVE FAITHS

I know stuff. Stuff I shouldn't. It scares some people.

Rosie O'Donnell

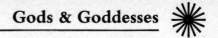

I have met a great many people on their way towards God and I wonder why they have chosen to look for him rather than themselves.

Jeanette Winterson

It seems to me that there is a great change come over the world since people like *us* believed in God. God is now gone for all of us. Yet we must believe and not only that we must carry out weakness and our sin and our devilish-ness to somebody.

Katherine Mansfield

The worst moment for an atheist is when he feels grateful and has no one to thank.

Wendy Ward

Now people don't believe in religion they are always looking for different ways to be.

Helen Fielding

I seriously determined to choose my own religion, instead of following blindly that which happened to be my father's. If this determination be sinful, I must still think it ever has been, and ever will be the sin of all intelligent minds.

Harriette Wilson

I wonder if other dogs think poodles are members of a weird religious cult.

Rita Rudner

Infernal Machinery

TECHNOLOGY HELL

Shortly after the turn of the century, America marshalled her resources, contracted painfully, and gave birth to the New Technology. The father was a Corporation, and the New Technology grew up in the Corporate image.

Alice Embree

We especially need imagination in science. It is not all mathematics, nor all logic, but it is somewhat beauty and poetry.

Maria Mitchell

Still, no matter how much the technology evolves, we have advanced very little in our human relationships and behaviour.

Lily Tomlin

Whatever the scientists may say, if we take the supernatural out of life, we leave only the unnatural.

Amelia Barr

For a list of all the ways technology has failed to improve the quality of life, please press three.

Alice Kahn

In studying the science of yesteryear one comes upon such interesting notions as gravity, electricity, and the roundness of the earth – while an examination of more recent phenomena shows a strong trend toward spray cheese, stretch denim and the Moog synthesizer.

Fran Lebowitz

What should you give a man who has everything?
A woman to show him how to work it.

Anonymous

COMPUTERS

They told me quite frequently that a computer could not write a programme; it was totally impossible; that all that computers could do was arithmetic ... that it had none of the imagination and dexterity of a human being.

Grace Murray Hopper

I was *so* grateful for the web, because most of the print magazines are utterly beholden to their advertisers.

Susie Bright

If it's really true what they say, that mine is the time-famished generation, then e-mail is our guilty snack, our comfort food.

Allison Pearson

The technology has allowed us to get into these faintly absurd situations where you're living thousands of miles from most of the people you love. And every now and then I think: what are we *doing?* We should all just live in villages!

Emma Donoghue

I love the way email confidences slip out and into the ether ... I'm not sure these confidences would be given in the flesh or on the telephone ... There's something very lovely about getting to know entire strangers purely through the medium of a shared concept.

Stella Duffy

Infernal Machinery

I don't see the proper home of the novel on the little screen. The book is a perfect form, a physical thing that you can carry with you, that survives power outages and doesn't need batteries. It's simple, it's aesthetically pleasing, and you can use it use again and again.

E. Annie Proulx

The C-drive on my (faulty) computer tells me every morning that it has spent the night de-fragmenting, and I feel sympathy with it.

Fay Weldon

I honestly believe computer games are the tools of the devil and that, when the Apocalypse does eventually come, everyone will be so engrossed with Sonic the Hedgehog that no one will heed the approaching hoof beats, and the horsemen trailing mighty engines of fire will trample us all to oblivion. So there.

Sue Arnold

It is the modern equivalent of nasty little boys ringing doorbells and running away.

Libby Purves on computer viruses

TELEPHONE

Men like phones with lots of buttons. It makes them feel important.

Rita Rudner

The cell phone has transformed public places into giant phone-a-thons in which callers exist within narcissistic cocoons of private conversations.

Mary Schmich

The telephone is a good way to talk to people without having to offer them a drink.

Fran Lebowitz

The phone company handles 84 billion calls a year – everything from kings, queens, and presidents to the scum of the earth.

Lily Tomlin, as Ernestine the Operator

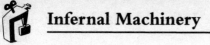

Infernal Machinery

You never know, it could be somebody important.

*The Queen, advising a young woman to answer her mobile phone
which rang while they were in conversation*

People harbour strange expectations about the telephone: they
expect you to use it! They expect you to answer no matter what
time it is, no matter what they're interrupting (they're always
interrupting *something*), whether you *like* them or not.

Lucy Ellman

Since mobile phones, lying has become much easier, much more
routine.

Barbara Ellen

Excuse me, everybody, I have to go to the bathroom. I really have
to telephone, but I'm too embarrassed to say so.

Dorothy Parker

I hold the telephone in reverence as an instrument of pure verbal
communication, and I don't like to see it messed about.

Lynne Truss

With a mobile in his hand, even the smallest rodent on the
corporate wheel starts to think he can act like a rock star.

Barbara Ellen

Mobile-phone bills have long replaced lipstick on the collar as
Exhibit A in cases of infidelity.

Barbara Ellen

The telephone is of real use only to important businessmen or to
women who have something to hide.

Colette

CARS

To attract men, I wear a perfume called "New Car Interior".

Rita Rudner

Infernal Machinery

Natives who beat drums to drive off evil spirits are objects of scorn to smart Americans who blow horns to break up traffic jams.

Mary Ellen Kelly

The first time I ever drove downtown, everything went wrong, and it wasn't my fault, none of it, it was my husband's fault … He had put the car in the garage backwards. Well, that shot the heck out of my map. Right away, I went out the wrong end of the garage.

Phyllis Diller

I used to have this great big Cadillac Escalade SUV that made me feel like a rap star, but I had to get rid of it because I couldn't reconcile owning it with my views on world oil dependence.

Gigi Levangie

There are two modes of transport in Los Angeles: car and ambulance. Visitors who wish to remain inconspicuous are advised to choose the latter.

Fran Lebowitz

TELEVISION AND RADIO

Radio and sex seem to me in a curious way not unalike. They are both enormous hidden empires, so to speak, existing all around us, but we only see their manifestations.

Ilka Chase

If I wished to be awakened by Stevie Wonder I would sleep with Stevie Wonder and that is why God invented alarm clocks.

Fran Lebowitz

We're so busy flicking channels these days that we miss the best programmes. The same can certainly be said for our relationships.

Mariella Frostrup

Television has proved that people will look at anything rather than each other.

Ann Landers

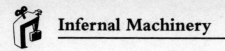

Infernal Machinery

We love television because television brings us a world in which television does not exist.

Barbara Ehrenreich

There are days when any electrical appliance in the house, including the vacuum cleaner, offers more entertainment than the TV set.

Harriet Van Horne

Gourmets & Garbage

FOOD HATES

How did people ever figure out that eggs were edible? Did they see something come out of a chicken and think, "Boy, I bet that would be tasty"?

Ellen DeGeneres

It is possible to eat English pie-crust, whatever you may think at first. The English eat it, and when they stand up and walk away, they are hardly bent over at all.

Margaret Halsey

One of my worst moments was when I drank my finger-dipping bowl at a royal party. I thought it was soup. Not only did I drink it, I also asked for the recipe.

Tara Palmer-Tomkinson

Isn't there any other part of a matzo you can eat?

Marilyn Monroe, on having matzo balls for dinner for the third time at Arthur Miller's parents'

Everything is organic – that means they didn't wash it.

Ruby Wax

Any dish that tastes good with capers in it, tastes even better with capers not in it.

Nora Ephron

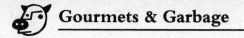# Gourmets & Garbage

A food is not necessarily essential just because your child hates it.

Katharine Whitehorn

Another thing I loathe but force myself to have is skimmed milk: it's like water that you've dipped your paintbrush into but it's got the calories stripped out of it, so I drink it.

Joan Rivers

Cocoa? Cocoa? Damn miserable puny stuff fit for kittens and unwashed boys. Did Shakespeare drink cocoa?

Shirley Jackson

A salad is not a meal. It is a style.

Fran Lebowitz

I hate salad. I put mushrooms in them because there is nothing in them, they're totally empty, like Britney Spears's head.

Joan Rivers

I was a vegetarian until I started leaning toward the sunlight.

Rita Rudner

I'll eat tuna, but only if it has that little sticker of the smiling dolphin with a slash through it. This means that the tuna is dolphin free. Actually, I'd like to see that sticker on other things because, frankly, I don't want dolphin in any of my food.

Ellen DeGeneres

The thing that children seem to enjoy most when eating out has got nothing to do with food. They love trooping backwards and forwards to the toilet.

Sue Townsend

FOOD FADS

Nutrition … has been kicked around like a puppy that cannot take care of itself. Food faddists and crackpots have kicked it pretty cruelly.

Adelle Davis

We are quick to despise what once we looked at so breathlessly in colour supplement and delicatessen. Just because a food is no longer flavour of the month, it shouldn't follow that it is evermore to be spoken of as a shameful aberration.

Nigella Lawson

The modern dieting religions (the ones which require a guru and a Bible rather than old-fashioned private self-control) are so specific that ... so much as a canapé in a non-believer's home. The very crockery is tainted.

Victoria Coren

Sneer, you *pâté de foies grasers!* But may you know the day when hunger will have you.

Edna Ferber

In New York it is now considered almost "hostile" according to *New York* magazine, to serve "carbs" at a party because everyone is on the Atkins diet.

Mary Killen

THE ART OF COOKING

Cooking is chic now. Cooking is sexy. Not being able to cook will soon be like not being able to drive.

Jeanette Winterson

I'm not a very good cook at all, it's amazing to admit it – it's like saying you're bad in bed or something.

Maeve Binchy

You could probably get through life without knowing how to roast a chicken, but the question is, would you want to?

Nigella Lawson

I like food, I like stripping vegetables of their skins, I like to have a slim young parsnip under my knife.

Stevie Smith

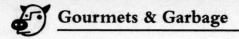

A leek is a scallion
Hung like a stallion.

Caryl S. Avery

It is hard to imagine a civilization without onions.

Julia Child

Herbs have strong psychological properties and can be used magically. They transform the way you think – they have an age-old resonance.

Titania Hardie

Cooking is like love. It should be entered into with abandon or not at all.

Harriet Van Horne

Non-cooks think it's silly to invest two hours' work in two minutes' enjoyment; but if cooking is evanescent, so is the ballet.

Julia Child

More than once I have been cured of mild depression by baking a cake.

Josceline Dimbleby

Men like to barbecue. Men will cook if danger is involved.

Rita Rudner

What's a chef? He's a protein pimp.

Ruby Wax

The Great Culinary Renaissance we hear so much about has done many things – given us extra virgin olive oil, better restaurants and gastroporn – but it hasn't taught us how to cook.

Nigella Lawson

Many people no longer cook, and simply buy cookery books as novels or as pornography.

Clarissa Dickson Wright

The great modernist dictum, Make It New, is not a helpful precept in the kitchen.

Nigella Lawson

The inexperienced think that if food is odd it must be a success.

Ruth Lowinsky

THE ART OF PRESENTATION

Thin, almost transparent slices of lemon do indeed go a long way in dressing up a meal but they should not be counted as a separate vegetable.

Fran Lebowitz

The Italians, from long poverty, by always putting "bella" before whatever insufficiency they have got to eat make it that much more appetizing.

Caitlin Thomas

If a man prepares dinner for you and the salad contains three or more types of lettuce, he is serious.

Rita Rudner

There is something aesthetic in the substance of a brown loaf.

Katherine Mansfield

The unwrapping of candy, like the opening of the shell of a pistachio nut, always increased my enjoyment of the meat therein by making me work for it.

Elaine Dundy

THE ART OF GLUTTONY

So much food,
So little time

Caryl S. Avery

There's nothing more sincere than the gratitude of a satisfied palate!

Liane de Pougy

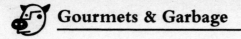

If I can't have a good meal, I'd rather skip it.

Candace Bushnell

If I can't have too many truffles, I'll do without truffles.

Colette

Everything you see I owe to spaghetti.

Sophia Loren

Elizabeth Taylor's so fat, she puts mayonnaise on aspirin.

Joan Rivers

My favourite animal is steak.

Fran Lebowitz

[The doctor] said I was the most sensitive person he had ever seen – that I belonged to the hyper-hyper type and we rarely survive! … They found that the eclair contains everything my system lacks. So I take three a day and I feel like a new woman.

Ruth Draper

I never felt my feelings, I just ate.

Sarah Ferguson, Duchess of York

FOOD AND FAMILY

Eating without conversation is only stoking.

Marcelene Cox

If an event is meant to matter emotionally, symbolically, or mystically, food will be close at hand to sanctify and bind it.

Diane Ackerman

Pinch not the guts of your family at home, that you may pamper yours abroad.

Hannah Woolley

Gourmets & Garbage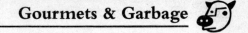

It's surely no coincidence that a large majority of anorexics report coming from homes in which fixed family mealtimes were sacrosanct, in which people had to eat whether or not they were hungry.

Julie Burchill

Family dinners are more often than not an ordeal of nervous indigestion, preceded by hidden resentment and ennui and accompanied by psychosomatic jitters.

M. F. K. Fisher

Kids who learn that they can tyrannize Mamma by refusing to eat often carry this mechanism into their adult lives.

Ann Landers

Family mealtimes are often little more than domestic abuse with a cherry on top.

Julie Burchill

When my mother asked me which part of the turkey I wanted, I said, "A wing please!" I really wanted breast, leg, or thigh. But wing was the only part of the bird without sexual connotations.

Sue Townsend's alter ego Adrian Mole

She wasn't a good cook, even by British standards of food in those days. The family called her puddings "Mrs Woodage's Revenge".

Elizabeth Jane Howard

My mother is such a lousy cook that Thanksgiving at her house is a time of sorrow.

Rita Rudner

Whenever I get married I start buying Gourmet Magazine.

Nora Ephron

If your husband wants to lick the beaters on the mixer, shut them off before you give them to him.

Phyllis Diller

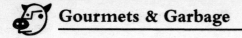

LIQUID SUSTENANCE

Alcohol makes people incoherent, sometimes permanently, but at least seems to make them more human than human, not less so.

Fay Weldon

Alcohol blows away your self-confidence, while at the same time allowing you to act as if you were the Queen of England.

Anne Robinson

For a good half of my professional life I didn't know where my next magnum was coming from.

Tallulah Bankhead

Not one man in a beer commercial has a beer belly.

Rita Rudner

The more glasses there are, the more "Mr Romantic Rights" there will be.

Caitlin Thomas

"Christmas drink" is a word like "duck", "lion" or "pheasant" that implies the plural.

Jilly Cooper

[When asked by Lucille Ball, "Could you be persuaded to have a drink, dear?"] "Well, maybe just a tiny triple."

Beatrice Arthur

It's OK for old people to drink really heavily at night, because they can go up to bed on that electric chair thing attached to the staircase.

Rhona Cameron

I like a glass of whiskey in the winter, I like a gin and tonic in the summer, I like a glass of champagne anytime.

Donna Tartt

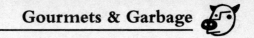

Whenever serious work is contemplated, the words "Time for a little something" spring immediately to mind.

Lynne Truss

Is There Intelligent Life Out There?

THE LIFE OF THE MIND

Intelligence is really a kind of taste: taste in ideas.

Susan Sontag

In the space age the most important space is between the ears.

Anne Armstrong

Whoever will cultivate their own mind will find full employment.

Lady Mary Wortley Montagu

The remarkable thing about the human mind is its range of limitations.

Celia Green

I believe there is so much more that we aren't aware of on a daily basis, that our abilities as human beings are so much vaster than we give ourselves credit for.

Gillian Anderson

I don't think about anything too much … If I think too much, it kind of freaks me out.

Pamela Anderson

Fifty per cent of the public don't actually know what the term fifty per cent means.

Patricia Hewitt

Is There Intelligent Life ...?

I know of no more pleasant feeling than suddenly to realize that you are intelligent.

Misia Sert

Intelligence and a great deal of it is a good thing to use when you have it it's all for the best.

Gertrude Stein

An orderly mind is a temple where truth condescends to appear, and delights to be worshipped.

Harriet Martineau

My dream now, in retrospect then, was to be an eclectic knowledge-gathering person, in order to be able to learn and then to teach.

Martha Stewart

I instinctively did all I could to make myself a personality to be reckoned with. For this reason I devoured books whatever their qualities, and fed my brain with the thoughts of dead men.

Marie Corelli

You can't ever be really free if you admire somebody too much.

Tove Jansson

Education is a thing that should never end with any of us till we are too old to grow any more.

Olive Schreiner

Prejudices, it is well known, are most difficult to eradicate from the heart whose soil has never been loosened or fertilized by education; they grow firm there, firm as weeds among stones.

Charlotte Brontë

Every woman's life is a series of exorcisms from the spells of different oppressors: nurses, lovers, husbands, juries, parents, children, myths of the good life, the most tyrannical despots can be the ones who love us the most.

Francine du Plessix Gray

Is There Intelligent Life ...?

LIFE & WORK

If Eve had had a spade in Paradise and known what to do with it,
we should not have had all that sad business of the apple.

Elizabeth von Arnim

We're a machine and we have to be worked in the same way we
have to be fed.

Twyla Tharp

Nothing will work unless you do.

Maya Angelou

To fulfil a dream, to be allowed to sweat over lonely labour, to be
given a chance to create, is the meat and potatoes of life. The
money is the gravy.

Bette Davis

My perfect day is to wake up feeling healthy, an idea in my brain, a
telephone in my pocket, and going out to be busy, constructive and
motivated.

Anouska Hempel

Work is a way of life for me and I've never resented a single hour
I've put into it.

Debbie Moore

I've got fantastic stamina and great physical strength, and I have a
woman's ability to stick to a job and get on with it when everyone
else walks off and leaves.

Margaret Thatcher

I catnap now and then, but I think while I nap, so it's not a waste of
time.

Martha Stewart

Recognize your gifts and delegate the rest.

Lynne Franks

Always aspire higher than you can. For, however high you aspire, you will never arrive more than halfway up the cliff of your aspiration.

Caitlin Thomas

I need to move all the time. I'm not nervous, I'm like a shark – I need to go forward to stay alive.

Monica Bellucci

Opportunities are usually disguised as hard work, so most people don't recognize them.

Ann Landers

What we are doing is just a drop in the ocean. But if that drop was not in the ocean, I think the ocean would be less.

Mother Teresa

You cannot be really first-rate at your work if your work is all you are.

Anna Quindlen

Full-on careers aren't as wonderful as people think.

Billie Piper

Our jobs take too much out of us and don't pay enough.

Anna Quindlen

I don't beg. I have not begged from the time we started the work. But I go to the people – the Hindus, the Mohammedans, and the Christians – and I tell them: "I have come to give you a chance to do something beautiful for God."

Mother Teresa

You don't have the right to give up, nor have you the right to say, "I've done enough."

Rabbi Julia Neuberger

I never think of age. I've no time. I work. Retirement? I don't know what that is. One works or one cannot work – that would be death.

Nadia Boulanger

Is There Intelligent Life ...?

Who said you should be happy? Do your work.

Colette

You feel that you're always living at the edge of making some very big mistake.

Condoleezza Rice

You may have to fight a battle more than once to win it.

Margaret Thatcher

WORK ETHICS

I'm trying to cast off those feelings of shame and sin through my work.

Madonna

Without our suffering, our work would be just social work.

Mother Teresa

Woman needs work more than work needs woman. The woman incapable of work always falls into degrading dependence in one form or another.

Ellen Key

My grandfather once told me that there were two kinds of people: those who do the work and those who take the credit. He told me to try to be in the first group; there was much less competition.

Indira Gandhi

I think it's good for the soul to do things where there's a good chance that you'll die a hundred times.

Daisy Donovan

I'm incredibly disciplined, too, thanks to having that work ethic drummed into me by my father.

Jade Jagger

You have to accept the treachery of the workplace. You cannot waste time discovering it daily. That's like saying every morning, "Oh! Traffic in London."

Anne Robinson

No matter who says what, you should accept it with a smile and do your own work.

Mother Teresa

AMBITION

To be successful, the first thing to do is fall in love with your work.

Sister Mary Lauretta

To follow, without halt, one's aim: that's the secret of success.

Anna Pavlova

Work makes me happy. If I'm in the race, I'm in the race to win, for myself. It's not about stepping on the next guy to step ahead. There's room for everybody. It's not as small a winners' circle as people think.

Halle Berry

I was never going to be a checkout girl.

Anne Robinson

I have no patience with women who ask permission to think.

Rosa Bonheur

New ideas are inspired by pressure.

Paloma Picasso

I get the childish tearful feelings over any "success" story or any "new beginning".

Antonia White

We are unfaithful to the dreams of our youth at our great peril, and the unfulfilled desires of our younger selves can make our older selves angry, bitter, and resentful.

Carolyn Miller

I don't think I will ever achieve my goals.

Ellen MacArthur

Is There Intelligent Life ...?

I'm a bitter ender.

Tallulah Bankhead

MEN & WOMEN IN THE WORKPLACE

Women ... don't feel called to mount a barrel and harangue by the hour every time they imagine they have produced an idea.

Anna Julia Cooper

Always suspect any job men willingly vacate for a woman.

Jill Tweedie

When people said to me, "Do you feel that you opened the door for these other women?" I had assumed that they were open and I was just walking through like everyone else.

Suzanne Vega

Women have a manifest advantage over men in doing business; everything smooths down before them, and to be a female is commonly sufficient to be successful, if she has a little spirit and a little common sense.

Hester Thrale

Not only have women been successful in entering fields in which men are supposed to have a more natural aptitude, but they have created entirely new businesses.

Lucretia P. Hunter

Frankly, asking a City woman if she has experienced sex discrimination is like asking a lamppost about its experience of dogs. The offence is so frequent that it scarcely seems worth commenting on.

Allison Pearson

In films beautiful girls in tortoiseshell spectacles and flat-heeled shoes are first humiliated for competing with men, then they are forgiven, loved, and allowed to be glamorous only when they admit their error.

Margaret Mead

Is There Intelligent Life …?

I don't know a single successful woman whose career trajectory hasn't in some part relied on, in no particular order, good dentistry, occasional artful display of cleavage/leg, faux-Luddite bemusement in the face of technology, and flirting. Not all the time, you understand, but on demand, when called for.

India Knight

The women's movement has made a huge difference … There are women doctors and women lawyers. There are anchorwomen, although most of them are blonde.

Nora Ephron

The hardest thing will be conceptually for us to start thinking of women as the ones who run things and letting go of the self-image that being a woman means being the reactor to events beyond our control.

Naomi Wolf

Toughness doesn't have to come in a pinstripe suit.

Dianne Feinstein

People are terrified when I ask them to come with me into a small room.

Martha Lane Fox

When I first arrived as a trainee in the City, I assumed that meetings were for making decisions; it took a few weeks to figure out that they were arenas of display, the Square Mile equivalent of those gorilla grooming sessions you see on wildlife programmes.

Allison Pearson

Whether he admits it or not, a man has been brought up to look at money as a sign of his virility, a symbol of his power, a bigger phallic symbol than a Porsche.

Victoria Billings

The power to get other people to do things has been the prerogative of the harlot throughout the ages – and of the manager.

Katharine Whitehorn

How you behave at office parties, however, should depend on how much you value your job.

Jilly Cooper

The Creative Urge

IRREPRESSIBLE CREATIVITY

An artist or writer is a specimen human being who just goes about the world hoping to be a bundle of nerve endings that take in everything and transform it into a voice.

Erica Jong

One of the most wicked destructive forces, psychologically speaking, is unused creative power ... the psychic energy turns to sheer poison. That's why we often diagnose neuroses and psychotic diseases as not-lived higher possibilities.

Marie-Louise von Frantz

I want to write, but more than that, I want to bring out all kinds of things that lie buried deep in my heart.

Anne Frank

I have this need to create something that affects people.

Jennifer Lopez

I can always be distracted by love, but eventually I get horny for my creativity.

Gilda Radner

I know that I'm a real writer because sometimes I write a short story just because I want to; not because someone's told me to.

Fay Weldon

The Creative Urge

Everyone has talent. What is rare is the courage to follow the talent to the dark place where it leads.

Erica Jong

Almost every artist has known this trauma of the breaking of the bridge to the world because you are creating another world.

Anaïs Nin

The world that you create just keeps getting more and more interesting.

Alice Walker

I always believed that artists were more in need of love than of respect.

Misia Sert

Lofty natures are not the most robust ... We are compressed in every way, and our roots and branches grow where and how they can. Thus, great *artistes* are often infirm, and several have been impotent.

George Sand

Perhaps the least cheering statement ever made on the subject of art is that life imitates it.

Fran Lebowitz

Art is the only thing that can go on mattering once it has stopped hurting.

Elizabeth Bowen

Writers are cannibals ... It is a terrible thing to be the friend, the acquaintance, [or] the relative of a writer.

Cynthia Ozick

Is it true that writers are pillagers of privacy? ... But what are a few hurt feelings along the fiction trail? After all, thousands died to build the railroads, millions were crippled and wounded in wars that were presumably fought to create better worlds.

Anne Roiphe

The Creative Urge

No writer should ever sleep with, live with or, God forbid, marry an aspiring writer – not without reading what happened to J. D. Salinger.

Amanda Craig

The clamour of "spotters" – friends, non-friends, critics, acquaintances and perfect strangers – on the scent or in the know is doubtless an occupational trial for writers of fiction … But in my case, I suppose because much of what I wrote dealt with romantic and sexual love seen from a subjective angle, the detective squads were rampant.

Rosamund Lehmann

Unless you are irresistibly shoved beyond all human control to create: pack it in.

Caitlin Thomas

Everywhere I go I'm asked if I think university stifles writers. My opinion is they don't stifle enough of them.

Flannery O'Connor

What I would say to a young person trying to become a writer is "Don't". It won't make any difference because they'll do it anyway, but they really shouldn't.

A. L. Kennedy

INSPIRATION & ORIGINALITY

The material's out there, a calm lake waiting for us to dive in.

Beverly Lowry

You can't simply go in for being an artist as such. You must wait to find something which excites you, fires your imagination, your desire, creates a real longing to do that one thing.

Bridget Riley

You never know if you're going to write another one. If nothing presents itself that's compelling, there's no point in just spinning your wheels.

Margaret Atwood

The Creative Urge

Invention, it must be humbly admitted, does not consist in creating out of voice, but out of chaos.

Mary Shelley

We live in an age of reinvention and it's important not to get artistically stale.

Dillie Keane

Could my ideas flow as fast as the rain in the storecloset, it would be charming.

Jane Austen

It is amusing to observe how the taste of a youngster, uninfluenced by others will form itself, grow away from tradition, grope for something new and different and thus discover the style of its own time. Suddenly there exists a whole new generation of such lonely explorers and a new art is born.

Vicki Baum

Another unsettling element in modern art is that common symptom of immaturity, the dread of doing what has been done before.

Edith Wharton

You don't make art by consensus.

Tracy Chapman

I love difference. I don't love the same. As soon as people start copying what I do – and they have – I move on.

Lulu Guinness

When you do subversion in a mainstream way, it's interesting.

Chloë Sevigny

Any authentic work of art must start an argument between the artist and his audience.

Rebecca West

Artists are meant to be madmen, to disturb and shock us.

Anne Rice

Finding a businessman interested in the arts is like finding chicken shit in the chicken salad.

Alice Neel

The unconscious artist who resides in our depths is a very economical individual. With a few symbols a dream can define the whole of one's life.

Doris Lessing

Art is the only way to run away without leaving home.

Twyla Tharp

MEMOIR & BIOGRAPHY

Hiring someone to write your autobiography is like paying someone to take a bath for you.

Mae West

Writing the story of your own life, I now know is … a bit like drilling your own teeth.

Gloria Swanson

Writing about your past is like blundering through your house with the lights fused, a hand flailing for points of reference.

Hilary Mantel

I HATE … biographies of *living* people. I always let people *invent* mine, & have often learnt some curious particulars about myself.

Elizabeth Gaskell

My new book is a memoir; aren't they all, this year?

Hilary Mantel

I've given my memoirs far more thought than any of my marriages. You can't divorce a book.

Gloria Swanson

Just how difficult it is to write biography can be reckoned by anybody who sits down and considers how many people know the real truth about his or her love affairs.

Rebecca West

The Creative Urge

In writing biography, fact and fiction shouldn't be mixed. And if they are, the fiction parts should be printed in red ink, the fact parts in black ink.

Catherine Drinker Bowen

THE PROCESS OF WRITING

The truth is we write for love. That is why it is so easy to exploit us.

Erica Jong

I seem to live while I write – it is life, for me.

Elizabeth Barrett

The use of language is all we have to pit against death and silence.

Joyce Carol Oates

The writer nevertheless has the good fortune to be able to escape his own petrifaction at the moments when he is writing.

Simone de Beauvoir

Writing, like making love, is more fun when you know what you're doing.

Eileen Jensen

The art of the novel happens because the storyteller's own experiences of men and things … has moved him to an emotion so passionate that he can no longer keep it shut up in his heart.

Murasaki Shikibu

I think and plot for years, and so when I sit down at the screen I expect to write as if taking dictation from the Holy Ghost.

Hilary Mantel

A woman writer has a double dose of masochism: the masochism of the woman and that of the artist.

Edna O'Brien

The Creative Urge

Writing is inevitably a solitary business: one lives inside one's own head to a degree, sometimes, that makes one scream at the terrible, monotonous inevitability of one's own thoughts and opinions.

Joanna Trollope

I have this nasty habit of writing every day; I feel unclean if I don't write.

Bernice Rubens

Writing only leads to more writing.

Colette

Excessive literary production is a social offence.

George Eliot

Writing is the only thing that when I'm doing it I don't think I should be doing something else.

Gloria Steinem

It's like a form of self-injury. Every time I write a book, I've probably taken five years off my life.

Rachel Cusk

I've finished by book … as usual it took days and nights of despair.

Colette

Novels don't go away, you can't sleep. You wake up and it's still there, this crevasse that goes on for miles, and it's dark but you have to go down there, and keep going down there.

Ali Smith

The *artiste* is an explorer who should allow nothing to daunt him.

George Sand

I really had to go through a pain barrier to find a slightly different writer in myself.

Esther Freud

No matter how things go, writers always have enough suffering to go around.

Siri Hustvedt

The Creative Urge

WORD BY WORD

In the writing process, the more a story cooks, the better.

Doris Lessing

One should be able to return to the first sentence of a novel and find the resonances of the entire work.

Gloria Naylor

Sit down and put down everything that comes into your head and then you're a writer. But an author is one who can judge his own stuff's worth, without pity, and destroy most of it.

Colette

It's a luxury to be able to abandon a story.

Lorrie Moore

I can't write five words but that I change seven.

Dorothy Parker

I keep going over a sentence. I nag it, gnaw it, pat and flatter it.

Janet Flanner

And there was that poor sucker Flaubert rolling around on his floor for three days looking for the right word.

Dorothy Parker

I ain't afraid of pushin' grammar around so long as it sounds good.

Mae West

I'm trying to wean myself off the punilingus. Trying. But I do love word play.

Kathy Lette

That's what they call a metaphor in our country. Don't be afraid of it, sir, it won't bite.

Emily Dickinson

It pleases me much more if someone says, "I love this sentence" than if someone says, "I loved your book".

Donna Tartt

TRUTH OR DARE

Fiction is like a spider's web, attached ever so lightly perhaps, but still attached to life at all four corners.

Virginia Woolf

Why, after all, should readers never be harrowed? Surely there is enough happiness in life without having to go to books for it.

Dorothy Parker

Great writers leave us not just their work, but a way of looking at things.

Elizabeth Janeway

I'm not what people call a "natural storyteller". That's a person who likes to be at the centre of a circle. I prefer lurking in a doorway, unnoticed.

Hilary Mantel

Characters are not created by writers. They pre-exist and have to be found.

Elizabeth Bowen

I can do to him whatever I like. I'm allowed to torture him as much as I want. He's mine.

J. K. Rowling on Harry Potter

When you write happy endings you are not taken seriously as a writer.

Carol Shields

Any writer overwhelmingly honest about pleasing himself is almost sure to please others.

Marianne Moore

The Creative Urge

I attribute my good fortune to the simple fact that I have always tried to write straight from my own heart to the hearts of others, regardless of opinions and indifferent to results.

Marie Corelli

The great thing about fiction-writing is that you are licensed to lie. There is no pleasure like it.

Victoria Glendinning

Write the truth and no one believes you: it's too alarming. So you might as well make it up.

Fay Weldon

I write about the world I was brought up in, a world where snobbery, hypocrisy and unquestioned conservatism are the norm. I just try and show it like it is, and God knows, that's damning enough.

Mary Wesley

You have to write about what you know. You wouldn't expect Jane Austen to write about Siberian peasants, she couldn't do it.

Nancy Mitford

I think I may boast myself to be, with all possible vanity, the most unlearned and uninformed female who ever dared to be an authoress.

Jane Austen

You can have no idea, if you have not tried, how difficult it is to find out anything whatever from an encyclopaedia, unless you know all about it already.

Gwen Raverat

The traditional advice to writers is "write what you kno.". I always amend that to "write what you can imagine knowing".

Elizabeth Forsythe Hailey

People may say that they don't like your novel, but they can't say you "got it wrong".

Victoria Glendinning

DISTRACTIONS

I've always thought people write because they are not living properly.

Beryl Bainbridge

In twenty years I've never had a day when I didn't have to think about someone else's needs. And this means the writing has to be fitted around it.

Alice Munro

The real pros are those like P. D. James who got up early every morning to write, before taking her children to school, going to work as a civil servant and looking after a sick husband. Only amateurs have temperaments that render them too delicate to take their kids swimming or to carry out the garbage.

Amanda Craig

I write in short paragraphs because when I began there were always children around, and it was the most I could do to get three lines out between crises.

Fay Weldon

It reached a point where I had to pretend I didn't know how to iron or I'd never have written anything at all.

Elizabeth Jane Howard

I cannot imagine an occupation more in conflict with writing than homemaking.

Paulette Childress White

I've spent so long erecting partitions around the part of me that writes … that I'm not sure I could fit the two parts of me back together now.

Anne Tyler

It's different for men, of course. They have wives making the coffee. My generation of women would never have felt you could sit up in your room and write. Far too selfish.

Beryl Bainbridge

The Creative Urge

The ideal view for daily writing, hour on hour, is the blank wall of a cold-storage warehouse. Failing this, a stretch of sky will do, cloudless if possible.

Edna Ferber

GETTING PUBLISHED

Even Nobel Laureates can benefit from the comments of a good editor.

Colleen McCullough

True creative freedom is these days reserved for children's authors, their editors silenced and their marketing departments struck dumb by the unexpected success of *Harry Potter*.

Fay Weldon

If somebody could write a book for people who never read they would make a fortune.

Nancy Mitford

Chick-lit is a deliberately condescending term they use to rubbish us all. If they called it slut-lit it couldn't be any more insulting.

Jenny Colgan

I am the only author with two hundred virgins in print.

Barbara Cartland

I make so much absorbing literature with such attractive titles and even if I could be as popular as Jenny Lind where oh where is the man to publish me in series … He can do me as cheaply and as simply as he likes but I would so like to be done.

Gertrude Stein

A person who publishes a book wilfully appears before the populace with his pants down.

Edna St Vincent Millay

Americans look at you very differently, respect you greatly more when you write a book. It doesn't even matter if it's good.

Martha Stewart

The Creative Urge

The best kind of fame is a writer's fame. Just enough to get a good table at a restaurant, and not enough for someone to interrupt you while you are eating.

Fran Lebowitz

If Shakespeare had to go on an author tour to promote *Romeo and Juliet*, he never would have written *Macbeth*.

Joyce Brothers

A single bad review of the book you publish during the research for the current one can temporarily blot out the sun.

Victoria Glendinning

Nothing induces me to read a novel except when I have to make money by writing about it. I detest them.

Virginia Woolf

An artist is born kneeling; he fights to stand. A critic, by nature of the judgment seat, is born sitting.

Hortense Calisher

Ideally we should have critics who are critics and not novelists who need to earn a bit to tide them over, or failed novelists.

Doris Lessing

READERS

I'm a lousy writer; a helluva lot of people have got lousy taste.
Grace Metalious, author of Peyton Place

Every time I write something, a little voice in my head says, "No one's going to read this." You have to be very stubborn to persist.

Joyce Carol Oates

Perhaps the most profound desire I entertain today is that people should repeat in silence certain words that I have been the first to link together.

Simone de Beauvoir

♪ The Creative Urge

But it would be sad if one's books were not the best of one, seeing that they reach farther and last (it is to be hoped) longer than the personality they went out from.

George Eliot

The best book is a collaboration between author and reader.

Barbara Tuchman

We write for all the world, for all who require to be initiated; when not understood, we resign ourselves to it and begin again. When understood, we rejoice and go on writing.

George Sand

Trust your reader, stop spoon-feeding your reader, stop patronizing your reader, give your reader credit for being as smart as you at least.

Hilary Mantel

The writer is always tricking the reader into listening to the dream.

Joan Didion

A well-composed book is a magic carpet on which we are wafted to a world that we cannot enter in any other way.

Caroline Gordon

I have found … that my subject in fiction is the action of grace in territory held largely by the devil. I have also found that what I write is read by audience which puts little stock either in grace or the devil.

Flannery O'Connor

One of the factors that contributes most to distorting writers' public images is the number of people who include us in their fantasy lives.

Simone de Beauvoir

There's still a strange moment with every book when I move from the position of writer to the position of reader, and I suddenly see my words with the eyes of the cold public. It gives me a terrible sense of exposure, as if I'd gotten sunburned.

Eudora Welty

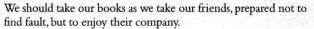

We should take our books as we take our friends, prepared not to find fault, but to enjoy their company.

Marie Corelli

Novels have turned my brain! No, no; I read novels because my brain is already turned.

Marie Bashkirtseff

I indulge, with all the art I can, my taste for reading. If I would confine it to valuable books, they are almost rare as valuable men. I must be content with what I can find.

Lady Mary Wortley Montagu

God forbid that any book should be banned. The practice is as indefensible as infanticide.

Rebecca West

WRITING & GENDER

Even the finest writers of each sex get the other sex wrong.

Amanda Craig

So much of Hollywood's use of sex and violence – from molten sex goddesses to larger-than-life action-adventure heroes – can be seen as an analogy to and even as a direct survival of Classical mythology.

Camille Paglia

In a book by a woman, rape won't be fun and women won't be simple-minded.

Marge Piercy

Women's virtue is man's greatest invention.

Cornelia Otis Skinner

The funniest thing is when men describe what they imagine sex must be like for a woman. As with John Cleland's pornographic masterpiece, *Fanny Hill,* there is always a lot about the stupendous role of the penis.

Amanda Craig

145

The Creative Urge

Women must leave a record for their men; otherwise how will they know us?

Sherley Ann Williams

I now wonder whether women can only get into a male character's head when he is cracked open by anguish.

Amanda Craig

Never despise what it says in women's magazines; it may not be subtle but neither are men.

Zsa Zsa Gabor

EROTICA

I mean, in my day, in a magazine, you didn't have sex, you had a row of dots.

Victoria Wood

There follows a little obscenity here, a dask of philosophy there, considerable whining overall, and a modern satirical novel is born.

Renata Adler

Erotica is simply high-class pornography; better produced, better conceived, better executed, better packaged, designed for a better class of consumer.

Andrea Dworkin

Erotica is to porn what a crocheted cover is to a toilet roll: deeply naff.

Julie Burchill

What pornographic literature does is precisely to drive a wedge between one's existence as a full human being and one's existence as a sexual being.

Susan Sontag

Feminist porn's absurd. I'm totally against it. I like regular porn.

Camille Paglia

I believe in censorship. I made a fortune out of it.

Mae West

POETRY

The poet is not an important fellow. There will always be another poet.

Stevie Smith

Poetry, "The Cinderella of the Arts".

Harriet Monroe

What the soul does for the body so does the poet for her people.

Gabriela Mistral

Poetry is like a strong explosion in the sky. She makes a mushroom shape of terror and drops to the ground with a strong infection.

Stevie Smith

If I feel physically as if the top of my head were taken off, I know that is poetry.

Emily Dickinson

MUSIC

Music takes me into another universe, ruled by necessity and composed of a substance, sound, which I find physically agreeable.

Simone de Beauvoir

Music at its greatest is for me an experience of the fourth dimension, that is, all human experience plus the extra one of *time*.

Janet Baker

At age ten I heard, for the first time, the singing of Marian Anderson on a recording. I listened, thinking, "This can't be just a voice, so rich and beautiful." It was a revelation. And I wept.

Jessye Norman

Going to the opera, like getting drunk, is a sin that carries its own punishment with it.

Hannah More

♪ The Creative Urge

Of all professions, surely singing is the most wonderful. I doubt if there exists a more intense joy than that experienced by a singer when she passes to her audience a little of her personal richness.

Edith Piaf

What, indeed, is more beautiful than to clothe one's feelings in sound, what a comfort in sad hours, what a pleasure, what a wonderful feeling, to provide an hour of happiness to others.

Clara Schumann

Music is a gift and a burden I've had since I can remember who I was.

Nina Simone

Musicals are movies that warn you by saying, "Lots of music here. Take it or leave it."

Fran Lebowitz

I still am good! I've got all the awards to prove it - plus nineteen Top Forty hits. The British public's simply not that gullible.

Cilla Black

I've been making a comeback but nobody ever tells me where I've been.

Billie Holiday

People say my voice is thin or small, but I have a lot more voice than I ever use. I ration it, and it's lasting very nicely.

Peggy Lee

The stronger songs have come in a cathartic way, as an expression of something that has been distilled over the years.

Annie Lennox

Composing a piece of music is very feminine. It is sensitive, emotional, contemplative. By comparison, doing housework is positively masculine.

Barbara Kolb

The Creative Urge

My family consists of pieces of work that go out into the world. Instead of hanging around for nineteen years they leave the nest early.

Joni Mitchell

The reason that some people don't like your music is the same reason that other people do.

Kirsty MacColl

You can't think, "I'm going to sit down and write a great song," and do it to order. I used to think that's what you had to do. A censor in my mind would go, "That's rubbish, throw it in the bin."

Annie Lennox

Writing songs is super intimate. It's a bit like getting naked.

Gwen Stefani

If I was singing about my deepest emotions, it would seem like a private joke. That's the music I write for myself. I get a lot out of it, but I just don't need to share it. It would almost be like I was raping myself. Why should I want to earn money off that?

Shania Twain

I love looking at my multicolored record sleeves, austere or gay, concealing such tumults and harmonies beneath their glossy surfaces.

Simone de Beauvoir

I love jazz. I think it's the only new thing in music in my lifetime.

Isak Dinesen

I will fight to the teeth anyone who says I am not an honest labourer for the art of music.

Maria Callas

I had to get rich in order to sing like I'm poor again.

Dolly Parton

My voice is my boss – it decides what is good and not good. I would never put it in a dangerous place.

Cecilia Bartoli

♪ The Creative Urge

I'm not sure where the notes come from sometimes. In the studio, I'm like: "I hope you saved that, 'cos it ain't coming out any time again today." Maybe they could get a dolphin in.

Mariah Carey

I don't really have time to sit down and write. But when I think of a melody, I call up my answering machine and sing it, so I won't forget it.

Britney Spears

The worst frustration for a singer is choosing a career in making music and then not being able to make music because you're always giving interviews.

Shakira

Pop music is the natural habitat of the supremely superficial.

Kirsty MacColl

THEATRE

To publish a novel or a poem one doesn't need to know print types or the publishing world. But to do a play ... one has to *know* the theatre.

Lillian Hellman

The theatre is a necropolis of ideas. One goes there to mourn the loss of life, and to numb the backside.

Rosalyn Drexler

I hate it. I find it incredibly tedious. I hate that it murders itself with its own conservative pomposity.

Fiona Shaw

That winter two things happened which made me see that the world, the flesh, and the devil were going to be more powerful influences in my life ... First, I tasted champagne, second, the theatre.

Belle Livingstone

The Creative Urge

Although one may fail to find happiness in theatrical life, one never wishes to give it up after having once tasted its fruits.

Anna Pavlova

The truth, the absolute truth, is that the chief beauty for the theatre consists in fine bodily proportions.

Sarah Bernhardt

Theatre risks every night. It has the possibility of soaring in the air or landing on its ass.

Anne Commire

Every now and then, when you're on stage, you hear the best sound a player can hear … a wonderful, deep silence that means you've hit them where they live.

Shelley Winters

No theatre is prosperous, or a play complete, unless there is a bedroom scene in the second act.

Daisy, Princess of Pless

Failure is faster in the theatre … more dramatic and uglier than in any other form of writing. It costs so much, you feel so guilty.

Lillian Hellman

It's one of the tragic ironies of the theatre that only one man in it can count on steady work – the night watchman.

Tallulah Bankhead

DANCE

Dance is the hidden language of the soul.

Martha Graham

When you perform … you are out of yourself larger and more potent, more beautiful. You are for minutes heroic. This is power. This is glory on earth. And it is yours nightly.

Agnes De Mille

People come to see beauty, and I dance to give it to them.

Judith Jamison

If you dance, you dance because you have to. Every dancer hurts, you know.

Katherine Dunham

As for that static ballroom mockery of dancing: of a couple of swooning codfish clasped together in a hazy trance; it is nothing but an excuse for an opportunity of mutual masturbation.

Caitlin Thomas

I regret the cheek-to-cheek dancing which has been replaced by wide spaces between partners. Each one dances *alone*.

Anita Loos

ART

Does it seem to you that it is possible to speak of Art? It would be the same as explaining love!

Eleonora Duse

Since I cannot sing, I paint.

Georgia O'Keeffe

Everybody's an artist. Everybody's God. It's just that they're inhibited.

Yoko Ono

Before I put a brush to canvas, I question, "Is this mine?"

Georgia O'Keeffe

I paint self-portraits because I am so often alone, because I am the person I know best.

Frida Kahlo

When I paint a picture I want to give a message and I care comparatively little about how good the art is.

Vanessa Bell

Art is not living. It is a use of living.

Audré Lorde

The Creative Urge ♪

I don't mind being miserable as long as I'm painting well.

Grace Hartigan

If I hadn't started painting, I would have raised chickens.

Grandma Moses

PHOTOGRAPHY

Blessed be the inventor of photography! It has given more positive pleasure to poor suffering humanity than anything else that has "cast up" in my time – this art by which even the "poor" can possess themselves of tolerable likenesses of their absent dear ones.

Jane Welsh Carlyle

A photograph is a secret about a secret. The more it tells you the less you know.

Diane Arbus

When we're afraid we shoot. But when we're nostalgic we take pictures.

Susan Sontag

For me the subject of the picture is always more important than the picture.

Diane Arbus

Excitement about the subject is the voltage which pushes me over the mountain of drudgery necessary to produce the final photograph.

Berenice Abbott

Cameras are a great leveller, cruel and flattering at once, like Uriah Heep with a chainsaw.

Joanna Lumley

I longed to arrest all beauty that came before me, and at length the longing has been satisfied.

Julia Margaret Cameron

♪ The Creative Urge

The camera makes everyone a tourist in other people's reality, and eventually in one's own.

Susan Sontag

CINEMA

The words "Kiss Kiss Bang Bang", which I saw on an Italian movie poster, are perhaps the briefest statement imaginable of the basic appeal of the movies.

Pauline Kael

Show me the story. I just want to tell a story that pulls me forward. Granted there are only seven stories in the universe. And I agree with that. But give me a great variation of those stories.

Debra Winger

I saw my first porno film recently – a Jewish porno film – one minute of sex and nine minutes of guilt.

Joan Rivers

When I see those ads with the quote "You'll have to see this picture twice", I know it's the kind of picture I don't want to see once.

Pauline Kael

Great directors have great egos. But they approach the work of genius with enormous humility.

Thelma Holt

THAT'S SHOWBIZ

I can't talk about Hollywood. It was a horror to me when I was there and it's a horror to look back on.

Dorothy Parker

The people are unreal. The flowers are unreal, they don't smell. The fruit is unreal, it doesn't taste of anything. The whole place is a glaring, gaudy, nightmarish set.

Ethel Barrymore

The Creative Urge

What I like about Hollywood is that one can get along by knowing two words of English – SWELL and LOUSY.

Vicki Baum

Where is Hollywood located? Chiefly between the ears. In that part of the American brain lately vacated by God.

Erica Jong

Showbiz has always been a honey-monster, chewing up and spitting out youthful pulchritude like the pips from cherries.

Julie Burchill

You go in and out with the breeze. That's Hollywood, after all. Certainly after I've done a film that everybody reacted to, I've felt that I've made an impact. Then you continue to float out to sea until the next wave catches you – or you catch it, as the case may be.

Sally Field

Suicide is much easier and more acceptable in Hollywood than growing old gracefully.

Julie Burchill

Hollywood is where they write the alibis before they write the story.

Carole Lombard

Hollywood follows polls like politics. They remake last year's hit.

Susan Sarandon

Hollywood money isn't money. It's congealed snow, melts in your hand.

Dorothy Parker

ACTING

I'm an actor! An actress is someone who wears boa feathers.

Sigourney Weaver

The Creative Urge

I feel a bit guilty for making such a good living out of something that I enjoy so much. Paid to dress up, pretend to be somebody, have all my friends around me, being part of a big gang, shouting and misbehaving …

Dawn French

Acting is a violent and intoxicating luxury, and I thrive on it.

Isabelle Adjani

If I'd been clever, I'd have been a sociologist or something, but I wasn't, so I became an actress.

Kristin Scott Thomas

If you're the type of actress that is researching and preparing, the camera getting turned on should just be a coincidence.

Debra Winger

I'd like to have been a really successful actress but I couldn't do it because I was too vain. As an actress people wouldn't have seen me as being intelligent.

Anne Robinson

I always wanted the world to be a movie. I wanted theme music when I walked down the street.

Winona Ryder

Film actors really do believe that lazing around a trailer all day having pancake applied until the time comes to utter one line is up there, physically and mentally, with coal mining in the 1800s.

Barbara Ellen

Acting's all about playing, and I'm a big kid.

Sienna Miller

What's so daunting is that you only have a small amount of time to depict a very powerful person, you know, with all her complexities, and how do you manage to put her essence on screen so quickly?

Nicole Kidman on playing Virginia Woolf in The Hours

The Creative Urge

You've got to be original, because if you're like someone else, what do they need you for?

Bernadette Peters

My husband asked, "Are you going to wear pointy ears?" I said, "Yes." He said, "Do it."

Cate Blanchett on playing an elf in The Lord of the Rings

The more flesh you show, the higher up the ladder you go.

Kim Basinger

People often say things like, "Why do you worry about your career stopping?" and I say, "Well, it's not unprecedented."

Julianne Moore

I've been typecast as a man-eater. But now I'm getting older I've got to surrender to Act Two and play the spurned woman instead.

Greta Scacchi

The French word for acting is *jouer* which also means to play – you should never lose sight of that.

Kristin Scott Thomas

Acting itself is not that complicated. It's surviving as a human being that's difficult. Having some taste and judgment and having a life.

Susan Sarandon

Not what you'd put on your Christmas list.

Anna Chancellor on doing sex scenes on film

After all these years, an actress still can't remove her top without the world going crazy. The film might involve her committing serial murder, robbing a pensioner or beating a child to the rhythm of an old Nazi anthem, but interviewers still ask only: "Did you have to think twice before taking your clothes off?"

Victoria Coren

I've made so many movies playing a hooker that they don't pay me in the regular way any more. They leave it on the dresser.

Shirley MacLaine

The Cult of Fame

THE MEDIA

I don't know which came first, the chicken or the egg? Were the people satanic and the media just reported on that?

Lily Tomlin

I once saw a Canadian reporter standing next to dead bodies making up his face. I was shocked at that.

Lara Logan

The tabloids are just porn that any kid off the street can go and buy for 50p.

Holly Valance

The media is now the real source of power.

Susan Faludi

Fame is a sound bite.

Erica Jong

The truth of the media is that first you're exploited and manipulated until you become this big balloon, which later they then puncture.

Kate Millett

I seem to live permanently in some kind of godawful soap opera.

Liz Hurley

Television has no regard for the absence or presence of talent: it merely makes you "famous".

Joanna Lumley

The Cult Of Fame

Television's another reason it's so hard to get started now as a comic … Unless you can do some dynamite thing like get caught with a hooker, have a murder in the family, or come back from dope, you know, people will just click, click, click right by.

Phyllis Diller

TV is fantasy, everyone knows that.

Nicola Griffith

In a way, the films *are* irrelevant. The stills and the press stories would have been enough.

Tina Brown on Brigitte Bardot

"Trying harder" in PR parlance is to produce a guest or an angle tailor-made for journalists whose investigative ethos is "follow that canapé".

Tina Brown

I suppose "talented" people have to work in advertising agencies and recording studios and they have to follow the rules and do what the boss says. But the world has never been changed by those people.

Lois Lowry

What is being promoted in adverts and magazines are not the things that make us like other people. You never see qualities like honesty, fun, or loyalty being promoted in adverts.

Helen Fielding

Is there anyone in the country who doesn't know how to be interviewed on television?

Rosie Millard

People used to throw Christians to the lions. Now they just throw them to the press.

Tammy Faye Bakker

I'm lucky that people have a negative conception of me: I can only look nice after that.

Sarah Ferguson, Duchess of York

In America it's about how you're seen. In Australia it's about how you feel. Here, it's more important to appear to be nice than to have heart.

Rachel Griffiths on the British media

In Hollywood, an equitable divorce settlement means each party getting fifty per cent publicity.

Lauren Bacall

Public opinion is a harlot which we ought to kick out of our way.

George Sand

There's a kind of sexism in the press, both highbrow and lowbrow, in Britain that you just can't get away with in any other English-speaking country.

Naomi Wolf

Oh, how I love to be interviewed! How I look forward to answering certain questions which have, since they've been asked so often, become like old friends, family even.

Bette Midler

What's nice about my dating life is that I don't have to leave my house. All I have to do is read the paper: I'm marrying Richard Gere, dating Daniel Day-Lewis … and even Robert De Niro was in there for a day.

Julia Roberts

Cicero has a great phrase for it: *aura popularis*, the popular breeze. It's all about which way the wind is blowing.

Donna Tartt

We are all soon forgotten; five minutes after I walk off the platform for the last time, I shall be forgotten.

Janet Baker

Hollywood has a very short memory.

Debra Winger

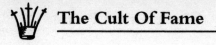

CELEBRITY

I mean, history is so short, but is it so compacted that I have to be an icon?

Deborah Harry

I stopped believing in Santa Claus at an early age. Mother took me to see him in a department store and he asked me for my autograph.

Shirley Temple Black

I've had moments when they've said, "Now it all begins." But it never begins ... hopefully it never quite ends.

Nicole Kidman

I was born at the age of twelve on a Metro-Goldwyn-Mayer lot.

Judy Garland

I am truly a product of Hollywood. I'm a product of Hollywood inbreeding. When two celebrities mate, I am the result.

Carrie Fisher

The fame you earn has a different taste from the fame that is forced upon you.

Gloria Vanderbilt

I've found the Nobel label very handy because who'd want to hear anything from Betty Williams, ordinary housewife?

Betty Williams, winner of the Nobel peace prize

Fame is always a misunderstanding of who you are.

Erica Jong

People think I'm some sort of strange Teletubby.

Björk

What does it mean when people applaud? ... Should I give 'em money? Say thank you? Lift my dress? The "lack" of applause – that I can respond to.

Barbra Streisand

The Cult Of Fame

I've had enough encounters with stars to know that they are as far from being normal as they are from being neuroscientists. They're all loonies, believe me.

Miranda Sawyer

I don't live with the celebrity thing. You just ignore it, and it ignores you.

Chrissie Hynde

I absolutely love it that the Queen has no idea who Madonna is.

India Knight

The more celebrity culture takes hold, the more names we have to add to the list: celebrity chefs and celebrity writers and celebrity gallery owners and celebrity lovers of other celebrities, and so on, and on, until there is no space left.

India Knight

It's lesbo-chic now, but what will be the taboo taste-thrill that ageing glamour girls have to admit to in ten years' time? Fancying dogs? Dead people? Dead dogs?

Julie Burchill

It's just fashion, isn't it? Being a Scot and a lesbian are two big handy ticks next to my name right now.

Ali Smith

Columbia sent me a telegram. It said simply, "America wants Lulu. Please send soonest."

Lulu

The public has a tendency to believe that our struggle for recognition begins when they hear of us for the first time. It never enters their head that we might have been fighting for years.

Edith Piaf

I can't tell you how many times I've been asked by people "Do you think race and gender contributed to your success?" How the heck do I know? I can't repackage myself as a white male and see whether I would have gotten this far.

Condoleezza Rice

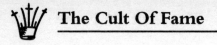

The Americans were slow to accept me but I bear no grudge.

Edith Piaf

FAME FLUNKIES

All fandom is a form of tunnel vision: warm and dark and infinite in one direction.

Zadie Smith

Manolo Blahnik … is destined to be a relentless pass-though character in the biographies of Bianca Jagger, Paloma Picasso, Jerry Hall.

Tina Brown

The more things you have, the more people you need to employ to look after them.

Billie Piper

At the Gap they have a special changing cubicle just for celebrities – it's just like all the others except it has a star on the door and a bowl of fruit inside.

Ellen DeGeneres

I can't go and get a coffee in Starbucks because the person behind the counter isn't going to hear me. He is just going to see something and become aware of every cell in his body at that moment. And I don't flatter myself, because it's got nothing to do with me. It's to do with this phenomenon of fame and our obsession with it in today's culture.

Renée Zellweger

I don't see myself certainly as a celebrity, as a star, because people are so familiar with me … Basically, people say "Hey, Oprah, come on over here and sit down." Every day, at the end of the show, they say, "Want to go to lunch, want to come to my house? I'm fixing so and so for dinner."

Oprah Winfrey

It is easier to play a big part than a small one.

Joanna Lumley

I always thought I'd go to the Oscars, but only as a stalker.

Rita Rudner

DIVADOM

I was a star. A real star – one of the kind who made the world important. I was the first and I was the best.

Pola Negri

Think of the Bible and Homer, think of Shakespeare and think of me.

Gertrude Stein

I would like to see the Pope wearing my T-shirt.

Madonna

Even as a twelve-year-old, I was saying, when am I going to become famous?

Mariah Carey

At thirteen, I would sit on the sink in the upstairs bathroom and pop my pimples, while having a conversation with Johnny Carson about the fact that when I was a kid, I used to sit on the sink in the upstairs bathroom and pretend to be talking to him.

Rosie O'Donnell

I used to narrate my life in headlines. I still do. When I was a kid, if I'd fall off a chair I'd announce, "Girl Falls off Chair."

Camille Paglia

I want to be more famous than anyone, ever. If it means I can't go to the shops without being mobbed, I won't mind.

Patsy Kensit

One of my first boyfriends said in an interview, "If Jennifer wasn't on TV right now, she'd be in Mexico singing in front of five people in a restaurant."

Jennifer Lopez

In rock, you are nothing until you've slept with Winona Ryder and had a feud with me.

Courtney Love

I am a nice person. I care about my driver having lunch, you know.

Barbra Streisand

I am who I am … If I'm on location in the woods and my trailer is miles away, I will go to the bathroom in the bushes … that's who I am.

Farrah Fawcett

I feel like a lion in the jungle.

Shakira

I'm an exhibitionist … I have a huge ego. I need attention.

Roseanne Barr

God, I can be difficult when I want to be.

Judi Dench

Unless you feel a million dollars, you're not going to perform a million dollars, which is what they should be paying you anyway, if you've negotiated properly.

Anne Robinson

I often wished to be more interesting, and less remarkable; *mais quoi faire?*

Harriette Wilson

I have too many fantasies to be a housewife … I guess I *am* a fantasy.

Marilyn Monroe

I always think that once you start talking about yourself in the third person you may as well just check into the clinic.

Nicole Kidman

After the holocaust, there will still be cockroaches and Cher.

Cher

If I fall, look out for the crash. There won't be anyone left standing.

Eva Peron

I behaved badly only because I felt superior to all who surround me.

Sarah Bernhardt

The nature of my life is a divadom, it really is. I don't do stairs.

Mariah Carey

It's a shame to call somebody a "diva" simply because they work harder than everybody else.

Jennifer Lopez

The word "diva" comes from the Latin "divus", meaning divine, meaning goddess, meaning a ball of demands, indulgence and whimsy wrapped in a glittering hard-as-nails shell.

Mimi Spencer

I'm not the public.

Lauren Bacall, on being told that a store was not open to the public

Egotism – usually just a case of mistaken nonentity.

Barbara Stanwyck

THE PRICE OF FAME

Beware of over-great pleasure in being popular or even beloved.

Margaret Fuller

Never, ever dream to presume.

Sarah Ferguson, Duchess of York

I had a famous grandfather, a famous father and mother, five famous uncles and twenty-eight famous cousins, so I wanted to do something that nobody else at home had done, and that was to work my way up to becoming a TV reporter.

Maria Shriver Kennedy

The Cult Of Fame

I was totally unprepared for the success of *Superwoman*. I was also totally unprepared for the blast of malice that accompanied its success.

Shirley Conran

When my first book came out, I was very confused. I was thrown into a world I knew nothing about. The metaphor that comes to mind is a shark tank.

Donna Tartt

If you have a big success, the next book is going to get trashed, whatever it is, because people are tired of your name.

Alison Lurie

I spent years of my life, though, to live it down. I was and remained "the girl who wrote *Grand Hotel*". It made me feel like a cat with a tin can tied to its tail.

Vicki Baum

Success has killed more men than bullets.

Texas Guinan

Fame is very uncomfortable, actually – it's incredibly alienating. The world turns you into stone, and treats you as an object.

Katharine Hamnett

You know, in China they say, "The thinner the chopsticks, the higher the social status." Of course, I got the thinnest I could find … that's why people hate me.

Martha Stewart

The sad truth is that excellence makes people nervous.

Shana Alexander

I don't want to be the star. Let them tear someone else a new butt!

Whoopi Goldberg

I get completely slagged off by people whose mortgage I'm paying. They write 500 words about me, they pay their mortgage that week.

Tracey Emin

On the outskirts of every agony sits some observant fellow who points.

Virginia Woolf

The second people stop paying $8.50 to see Tom Cruise there's no Tom Cruise. Tom Cruise lives at the *whim* of the audience. *That's* the price of fame, $8.50.

Fran Lebowitz

I do not pity Joan of Arc: that heroic woman only paid the price which all must pay for celebrity in some shape or other: the sword or the faggot, the scaffold or the field, public hatred or private heart-break.

Anna Jameson

The worst part of having success is to try finding someone who is happy for you.

Bette Midler

Winning it changed my life but the problem with that is that now "Pulitzer Prize winner" is almost a part of my name, and it seems to imply that my work has value only because of this prize.

Alice Walker

This publicity, these lights, this is also a form of humiliation. I accept this, as I did the Nobel Prize, only as a recognition of the poor.

Mother Teresa

I WANT TO BE ALONE

I've never looked through a keyhole without finding someone was looking back.

Judy Garland

Some days it seems like I have a light on my head wherever I go.

Halle Berry

The freedom of the press works in such a way that there is not much freedom from it.

Princess Grace of Monaco

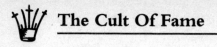 # The Cult Of Fame

There is a conflict between public and private life, and it's a conflict that I think ought to remain a conflict.

Toni Morrison

My private life is now private.

Patsy Kensit

There's no law that says any person of famous or semi-famous stature or reputation shall find it incumbent upon said person or personage to divulge eating, cooking, laundry, or animal-telepathy habits to general public at large.

Ellen DeGeneres

One doesn't have to answer the phone.

Donna Tartt

$

Material Girls

MONEY, MONEY, MONEY

If you want to know what God thinks of money, just look at the people he gave it to.

Dorothy Parker

The only people who claim that money is not important are people who have enough money so that they are relieved of the ugly burden of thinking about it.

Joyce Carol Oates

The poor wish to be rich, the rich wish to be happy, the single wish to be married, and the married wish to be dead.

Ann Landers

The richest people feel the sorriest for themselves.

Tama Janowitz

I hate almost all rich people, but I think I'd be darling at it.

Dorothy Parker

There is a tremendous preoccupation in this country with the rich. It's absurd. Relative to the population as a whole there are practically no rich people. It's like worrying about what to do with the geniuses. You're not going to meet any – forget about them.

Fran Lebowitz

With the refined indifference of the habitual money holder goes a congenital streak of acute meanness.

Caitlin Thomas

Being tight is the halitosis of human relations – unforgivable, unforgettable and totally incurable.

Barbara Ellen

If all the rich men in the world divided up their money amongst themselves, there wouldn't be enough to go round.

Christina Stead

Mick is avoiding taxes in every country in the world and he has thirteen lawyers helping him to do it.

Bianca Jagger

If you want to say it with flowers, a single rose says: "I'm cheap!"

Delta Burke

People who think money can do anything may very well be suspected of doing anything for money.

Mary Pettibone Poole

Some people think they are worth a lot of money just because they have it.

Fannie Hurst

Talking today of different kinds of Virtue I observed that Liberality among Virtues is as the Honeysuckle among Plants – profuse of its Fragrance and perfuming the Air all around it.

Hester Thrale

It used to be that cash bore some relation to refinement or taste, but this is no longer the case. Having money, it would seem, is now simply about having money.

India Knight

The two most beautiful words in the English language are: "cheque enclosed".

Dorothy Parker

Though I do not understand money, I love it as one does a complex and alluring Lothario.

Ilka Chase

Girls just want to have funds.

Adrienne E. Gusoff

I'd like to have money. And I'd like to be a good writer. These two can come together, and I hope they will, but if that's too adorable, I'd rather have the money.

Dorothy Parker

Some people get so rich they lose all respect for humanity. That's how rich I want to be.

Rita Rudner

For, far from becoming more spiritual as one gets older as is generally supposed, I have become a caterwauling virago of fanatical materialism. A dedicated cash-counter in the cellar by candlelight: Uriah Heep isn't in it, I can tell you.

Caitlin Thomas

True, I always shout "Buns for tea!" when a cheque arrives in the post.

Lynne Truss

Money is like sex. It is like food. They are all manifestations of God.

Madonna

I really was to the manor born. God got it so wrong by bringing me up in an estate in Hounslow. He really meant to put me on an estate in Gloucestershire.

Patsy Kensit

The nice thing about living in Gloucestershire is that none of us have our curtains made by people who haven't got a title.

Anne Robinson

I always like it when they mess up and say that I've earned more than I earn.

Madonna

EARLY LEARNING

There is always something your best friend had that you didn't have but really wanted.

Christy Turlington

I hate Barbie ... my inner anti-capitalist hates the global corporation of the brand; yes, my inner feminist despises the impossible body aesthetic which is forced on to young girls at an impressionable age; and yes, my friend Danielle owned a Barbie while I had to make do with the cheap knock-off doll which had only two outfits and no horse.

Victoria Coren

The easiest way for your children to learn about money is for you not to have any.

Katharine Whitehorn

If it weren't for baseball, many kids wouldn't know what a millionaire looked like.

Phyllis Diller

If I didn't have some kind of education, then I wouldn't be able to count my money.

Missy Elliott

When fourteen-year-old Tatum O'Neal was making the film *International Velvet*, a school inspector found her mathematical abilities somewhat lacking, and asked if it bothered her. O'Neal replied: "Oh, no, I'll have an accountant."

New York Times

Figures tinkle against my mind and drop off, like gravel hitting a barn-door, and financially I live in utter darkness.

Margaret Halsey

I was the original girl who thought that when there were cheques in the book there was money in the account.

Ilka Chase

WOMEN AND MONEY

Every woman should have a purse of her own

Susan B. Anthony

Having money is rather like being a blonde. It is more fun but not vital.

Mary Quant

I make money using my brains and lose money listening to my heart.

Kate Seredy

We women ought to put first things first. Why should we mind if men have their faces on the money, as long as we get our hands on it?

Ivy Baker Priest

Women and wealth is the last taboo.

Erica Jong

If one is rich and one's a woman, one can be quite misunderstood.

Katharine Graham

Where large sums of money are concerned, it is advisable to trust nobody.

Agatha Christie

A fool and her money are soon courted.

Helen Rowland

WHAT MONEY CAN'T BUY

Nothing buys happiness, but money can certainly hire it for short periods.

Irma Kurtz

To own is not to possess. To possess things needs a certain strength of soul; to own them, it is enough to be rich.

Marie d'Agoult

To me, "successful" is getting to the point where you are absolutely comfortable with yourself. And it does not matter how many things you have acquired.

Oprah Winfrey

I hate the noise and hurry inseparable from great estates and titles, and look upon both as blessings that ought only to be given to fools, for 'tis only to them that they are blessings.

Lady Mary Wortley Montagu

You pay for the outside crust of life, besides for the available inside goose-pie.

Elizabeth Barrett Browning

You must have some money if you are going to live simply.

Stevie Smith

THE ART OF SHOPPING

Shopping with an empty purse has by no means the relish and savour of shopping with a full one.

Mary Russell Mitford

A credit card is a money tool, not a supplement to money.

Paula Nelson

It was time to get in touch with my Inner Wallet.

Kathy Lette

Price-tag hunting is a favourite indoor sport.

Renee Long

If men liked shopping, they'd call it research.

Cynthia Nelms

Most men hate to shop. That's why the men's department is usually on the first floor of a department store, two inches from the door.

Rita Rudner

Men always claim that women are hard to give presents to. I'm dead easy – all I want is cashmere jerseys, in any colours except red, orange, maroon, fuchsia pink and custard yellow; silk shirts in ditto; jewellery; records; books; scent; gardening tokens and the man who plays Jeff Colby in *Dynasty*.

Jilly Cooper

These days I shop like a locust: famished, ruinous, hoovering up anything I need and things I definitely won't need but deserve, anyway, because I never have time to go shopping.

Allison Pearson

Anyone seeing women at a bargain-basement sale … sees aggression that would make Attila the Hun turn pale.

Estelle Ramey

I take Him shopping with me. I say, "OK, Jesus, help me find a bargain."

Tammy Faye Bakker

Look, I grew up in a goddamn shack, so I like a bit of comfort.

Mariah Carey

I was born ostentatious. They will list my name in the dictionary someday. They will use "Imeldific" to mean ostentatious extravagance.

Imelda Marcos

RICH & POOR

The poor do not need our condescending attitude or our pity.

Mother Teresa

Almsgiving leaves a man just where he was before. Aid restores him to society as an individual worthy of all respect and not as a man with a grievance. Almsgiving is the generosity of the rich; social aid levels up social inequalities.

Eva Peron

Whenever I watch TV and see those poor starving kids all over the world, I can't help but cry. I mean I'd love to be skinny like that but not with all those flies and death and stuff.

Mariah Carey

Rich people plan for four generations forward and poor people plan for Saturday night.

Gloria Steinem

Never make the unpardonable error, then, of thinking that it is romantic to be poor.

Caitlin Thomas

It is one thing to sin in charming surroundings after a delicious dinner with dry champagne and a crackling fire and the Hungarian gipsy records playing softly on the gramophone and quite another to resort to cheap hotels and the parked car.

Ilka Chase

I could not have money in the bank while people were starving.

Mother Teresa

You're not really poor until you put water on the cornflakes.

Elaine Markson

I was working in a bank and this lady said to me, "Never forget you're two pay cheques away from being homeless." That put the fear of God in me. Work hard, don't lose focus.

Jennifer Lopez

I am not surprised, all the same, or particularly shocked, when the poor steal from the rich. There is such a shortage of nice things at the bottom end of the ladder, and such a plethora at the top.

Fay Weldon

The other day I dreamed that I was at the gate of heaven. And St Peter said, "Go back to Earth, there are no slums up here."

Mother Teresa

The Dictators & The Downtrodden

HUMAN RIGHTS

Humanity wasn't obviously a made-to-order thing. It's a continuous struggle.

Rebecca West

Only as an egg in the womb are we all equal.

Oriana Fallaci

I recognize no rights but *human* rights.

Angelina Grimké

Dictatorship has a terrible effect on human reason.

Rose Macaulay

What is happening to women is happening to the whole world.

Anaïs Nin

Racism isn't as simple as the word used to describe it.

Alexandra Fuller

In this country American means white. Everybody else has to hyphenate.

Toni Morrison

There is no birthright in the white skin that it shall say that wherever it goes, to any nation, amongst any people, there the people of the country shall give way before it.

Annie Besant

The received (but not much acknowledged) TV wisdom is that it is not quite so embarrassing to journalist or viewer when the suffering group looks a bit different from us ... The less the resemblance to the life we know, the easier it is to intrude and to inspect.

Kate Adie

When you are captive you are very vulnerable, forever putting on a brave face but all the time facing your private fears.

Aung San Suu Kyi

The only way you can run a society that feels fair is to say that individuals with whom you disagree have a right to express their views.

Rabbi Julia Neuberger

There is practically nobody willing to identify themselves as American anymore because everybody is too busy identifying themselves with the area of their lives in which they feel the most victimized.

Fran Lebowitz

When people are aware of their rights, we would like them to be aware also of their responsibility.

Indira Gandhi

Injustice makes villains of us all.

Elizabeth Forsythe Hailey

Justice is better than chivalry if we cannot have both.

Alice Stone Blackwell

It doesn't matter where we begin the personal/political circle, but it matters desperately that we complete it.

Gloria Steinem

Revolution is the festival of the oppressed.

Germaine Greer

When anything gets freed, a zest goes round the world.

Hortense Calisher

HELL-RAISING

Get it right. I'm not a humanitarian. I'm a hell-raiser.

Mary Harris "Mother" Jones

Don't be a marshmallow. Walk the street with us into history. Get off the sidewalk. Stop being vegetables. Work for Justice.

Dolores Huerta

A passive person is not listened to. The loud wheel gets the oil.

Maya Angelou

Powerlessness and silence go together.

Margaret Atwood

People said, "I have a new voice because I'm gay, black, working-class." Nonsense. The only way is to chip away the accretions of cliché we all go around with.

Pat Barker

We have too many high sounding words, and too few actions that correspond with them.

Abigail Adams

If you think you're too small to have an impact, try going to bed with a mosquito.

Anita Roddick

There are revelations that are revolutions.

Marie d'Agoult

Because of 9/11 … Public citizens in America have no voice any more. You can't express an opinion without being considered a traitor … A conspiracy theory about UFOs now wouldn't be of interest, and what would be of interest would be too close for comfort.

Gillian Anderson

The argument of the broken pane of glass is the most valuable argument in modern politics.

Emmeline Pankhurst

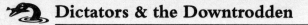

The common good is usually not very.

Fran Lebowitz

Every society honours its live conformists and its dead
troublemakers.

Mignon McLaughlin

The only possible way there'd be an uprising in this country would
be if they banned car boot sales and caravanning.

Victoria Wood

POLITICS

This is a democracy. We *are* the government ... I wish we weren't. I
wish there were a bunch of really smart people who were the
government, and *you weren't* the government. But, unfortunately,
you are.

Fran Lebowitz

Ninety-eight per cent of adults in this country are decent, hard
working, honest Americans. It's the other two per cent that get all
the publicity. But then, we elected them.

Lily Tomlin

I just think it's really wise to be informed and smart and not be
swept up in this sort of crazy fake patriotism that's just a deflection
for the present government to send people off the track of their
corruption.

Sandra Bernhard

Men are too emotional to vote. Their conduct at baseball games
and political conventions shows this.

Alice Duer Miller

Loneliness is the last great taboo. If we don't accept loneliness, then
capitalism wins hands down. Because capitalism is all about trying
to convince people that you can distract yourself, that you can
make it better. And it ain't true.

Tilda Swinton

Unless we change our ways and our direction, our greatness as a nation will soon be a footnote in the history books.

Margaret Thatcher

Politics, as everybody ought to know, are the most boring subjects on earth: causing the ears of the listener to snap shut with an involuntary click. The reason being, I think, that they are a biased playing off of one prejudice against another so that one never gets at the basic truth underneath.

Caitlin Thomas

If voting changed anything, they'd make it illegal.

Emma Goldman

Democracy is not an easy form of government, because it is never final; it is a living, changing organism, with a continuous shifting and adjusting of the balance between individual freedom and general order.

Ilka Chase

I don't think you ever manage to deal with politics. You just cope with it.

Zola Budd

Standing in the middle of the road is very dangerous; you get knocked down by traffic from both sides.

Margaret Thatcher

Liberals are just as fearful as reactionaries; for every Disgusted of Tunbridge Wells, there is a Horrified of Hampstead.

Julie Burchill

Aged sixteen, I was lying in bed, polishing the first poem I ever wrote, when our flat was raided by people who believed my father to be unsound. I had to tear up the poem and flush it down the toilet. I remember thinking: if this is a socialist paradise, what is hell?

Jung Chang

They say that women talk too much. If you have worked in congress you know that the filibuster was invented by men.

Clare Boothe Luce

Some say our foreign policy is all style and no substance, but they are just jealous of my hats and pins.

Madeleine Albright

Do I have an option?

Patricia Schroeder when asked by the press if she was "running as a woman"

If you run for office you spend about eighty per cent of your time begging for money. It takes a psychopathic personality to be willing to do that. American elected office had become a tomb for ideas.

Arianna Huffington

Oral sex in the Oval Office is not a priority.

Phyllis Chesler

Had Mr Clinton spent less time with voluptuous girls, had he made smarter use of the Oval Office, maybe September 11 would not have occurred.

Oriana Fallaci

George W. Bush's email address is president@whitehouse.gov. When you email him, they send you back these wonderful messages, like "President Bush will consider your email". Will he shit, he won't even see it. But then they know where your computer is and you're on their hit list.

A. L. Kennedy

WAR AND TERRORISM

You can no more win a war than you can win an earthquake.

Jeannette Rankin

The first victory is the avoidance of war.

Indira Gandhi

The statistics of the Holocaust are a ledger of evil, its entry figures still visibly tattooed on people's arms.

Nadine Gordimer

Everything, everything in war is barbaric.

Ellen Key

War: The male's normal compensation for not being female, namely, getting his Big Gun off, is grossly inadequate, as he can get it off only a very limited number of times; so he gets it off on a really massive scale.

Valerie Solanas

I hate it as the pacifists in bad or good faith never will. I loathe it. I hate it so much that every book I have written overflows with that loathing, and I cannot bear the sight of guns.

Oriana Fallaci

In the 60s we fought for peace, when the Vietnam war was on. We were against the cops and against the politicians … just as they were enjoying that machoism of war, we were enjoying the machismo of being anti-war … We cannot enjoy the machoism of fighting for peace.

Yoko Ono

What a country calls its vital economic interests are not the things which enable its citizens to live, but the things which enable it to make war. Petrol is more likely than wheat to be a cause of international conflict.

Simone Weil

I don't want to pay money for the shit heads who are buying armaments around the world. Every time a missile goes overhead I look up and think, "I bought the wing."

Erica Jong

There are two kinds of imperialists – imperialists and bloody imperialists.

Rebecca West

That is perhaps the ultimate more horrible demand of war; the State must have your conscience.

Stevie Smith

But the worst barbarity of war is that it forces men collectively to commit acts against which individually they would revolt with their whole being.

Ellen Key

It is a foolish delusion to believe that we need only live through the war, as a rabbit hides under the bush to await the end of a thunderstorm, to trot merrily off in his old accustomed gait when all is over,

Rosa Luxemburg

Because of [Hitler] not only do millions of people die but millions will not be born.

Ilka Chase

When there is a war the years are longer that is to say the days are longer the months are longer the years are much longer but the weeks are shorter that is what makes a war.

Gertrude Stein

Peace is when time doesn't matter as it passes by.

Maria Schell

War has become a luxury that only small nations can afford.

Hannah Arendt

We have to seek meaning in those who commit acts of terrorism, just as we do in the lives and deaths of their victims.

Nadine Gordimer

A war on terrorism implies that you are going to exterminate terrorism, and I don't see how anyone can do that. It's like exterminating evil. It can't be done.

Stella Rimington, former head of MI5

The greatest danger of our time is fundamentalist zealotry.

Erica Jong

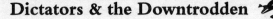

No one won the last war, and no one will win the next war.

Eleanor Roosevelt

THE WOMEN'S MOVEMENT

The prolonged slavery of women is the darkest page in human history.

Elizabeth Cady Stanton

In my heart, I think a woman has two choices: either she's a feminist or a masochist.

Gloria Steinem

We woman suffragists have a great mission – the greatest mission the world has ever known. It is to free half the human race, and through that freedom to save the rest.

Emmeline Pankhurst

> What a Woman may be, and yet not have the Vote
> Mayor Nurse Mother Doctor or Teacher Factory Hand
> What a Man may have been, and yet not lose the Vote
> Convict Lunatic Proprietor of White Slaves Unfit for Service
> Drunkard

Suffragette poster, c. 1901

If women want any rights more than they's got, why don't they just take them, and not be talking about it?

Sojourner Truth

To me the feminist movement is about not defining yourself simply by your ovaries.

Susan Faludi

In many languages, there is a single word for "wife" and "woman". Perhaps we should be thankful that English is no longer one of them.

Susan Maushart

I would have girls regard themselves not as adjectives but as nouns.

Elizabeth Cady Stanton

We had to fight for every inch of consciousness and dignity.

Phyllis Chesler

I don't think women are going to go back. There's been a threshold that we've crossed.

Susan Faludi

I've smashed my way through a good many barriers I never knew existed.

Shirley Conran

I want women to be liberated and still be able to have a nice ass and shake it.

Shirley MacLaine

Women should be tough, tender, laugh as much as possible, and live long lives. The struggle for equality continues unabated, and the woman warrior who is armed with wit and courage will be among the first to celebrate victory.

Maya Angelou

Many women do not recognize themselves as discriminated against; no better proof could be found of the totality of their conditioning.

Kate Millett

If what I do prove well, it won't advance.
They'll say it's stolen, or else it was by chance.

Anne Bradstreet

Women were ultimately designed for something better, though they have so long fared otherways.

Mary Anne Radcliffe

Until the day arrives when all women decide that our rights are not negotiable, our future choices will not be secure.

Faye Wattleton

Dictators & the Downtrodden 🐉

In the heat of the battle, women and feminists behave as badly as do non-comrades. We are not trained to give women even one more chance. We need to get more realistic as to what we can expect from women.

Phyllis Chesler

Understand: every attack on Hillary Clinton for not knowing her place is an attack on you. Underneath almost all those attacks are the words: get back, get back to where you once belonged.

Nora Ephron

I think those women that invented women's lib – which I never thought I was part of and don't think I am today – were very strident and harsh and aggressive and I think what they did was not win because you don't catch flies with vinegar, as my mother always said.

Barbara Taylor Bradford

If we can't laugh at ourselves without having a panic attack about what it says about women, we haven't got very far with our equality.

Helen Fielding

Being a feminist is not saying we are all the same.

Candace Bushnell

True, the movement for women's rights has broken many old fetters, but it has also forged new ones.

Emma Goldman

Where women are trapped today, there is no door to slam.

Naomi Wolf

My feminist generation ate our leaders.

Phyllis Chesler

It's hard to know what recent feminism is. There are no party headquarters, it's just a feeling.

Fay Weldon

MEN AS OPPRESSORS

Men refused to allow woman to raise herself in her own eyes.

George Sand

Needing to feel that women are inferior is a great weakness.

Anaïs Nin

Even though men in many places have deprived our sex of its share of the best advantages, this larceny and the suffering it causes is clearly due to the difference in physical strength rather than to a lack of mental capacities or moral worth on our part.

Marie de Gournay

Female size, especially brain size, has always been held to explain their unfitness for this or that ... until it was found that elephants' brains were even larger than men's.

Katharine Whitehorn

Freud, living at a time when women were proving their heads were no different from men's, substituted the penis for the head as the organ of male superiority, an organ women could never prove they had.

Una Stannard

Men feel that women's gain is their loss and I don't think that's at all true. It's more that men look around to explain their losses and fasten on women.

Susan Faludi

All I ask of our brethren is that they will take their feet from off our necks, and permit us to stand upright on that ground which God designed us to occupy.

Sarah Moore Grimké

In the USA, women are labelled, shackled, degraded, abused, humiliated. Men are coddled, protected, even patted on the back.

Heidi Fleiss

Men have it easier. Sometimes we have to overcome more things to get something done. And men know it! They *know* they don't facilitate those things for us. They're always: "Hey! We never supported this group of humans! How have they been able to do that? Because I know we tried *everything* possible to stop them!"

Salma Hayek

Daily Mailville, where men live their lives in a permanent state of terror that somehow, somewhere, *a woman may be having fun!*

Julie Burchill

Since God chose his spouse from among women … not only should men refrain from reproaching women, but should also hold them in great reverence.

Christine de Pisan

Men feel that women are on this great adventure, that women have a direction, that women, and I think this is true, have completely overhauled their notion of what it means to be female, what their role and identity is in society.

Susan Faludi

Beware the bearded academic feminist. They'll have you washing up the wok while they read Marx with a glass of rough red.

Mandy Saloman

Their terms for women in the '70s in Sydney were "bush pigs", "swamp hogs" or "maggots" and if you were good-looking, they called you a "glamour maggot".

Kathy Lette

MEN ARE NOT ALWAYS THE ENEMY

All this pitting of sex against sex, of quality against quality; all this claiming of superiority and imputing of inferiority, belong to the private-school stage of human existence where there are "sides", and it is necessary for one side to beat another side.

Virginia Woolf

I don't do that whole he's-a-man-I'm-a-woman, I've-got-a-hard-deal thing.

Sharleen Spiteri

I blame women for the way things are. Men aren't going to change because they don't have to.

Tama Janowitz

It's no use blaming the men – we made them what they are – and now it is up to us to try and make ourselves the makers of men – a little more responsible.

Nancy Astor

Some women are fiercely patriarchal. Some men are fiercely feminist.

Phyllis Chesler

Men of sense in all ages abhor those customs which treat us only as the vassals of your sex.

Abigail Adams

I mean what's the big deal about men being horrible to you?

Jo Brand

Men are not the enemy, but the fellow victims. The real enemy is women's denigration of themselves.

Betty Friedan

When women claim to feel cheated or betrayed by the feminist cause because they say, "I have a job and a man and I'm not happy", well that's not feminism's responsibility.

Susan Faludi

I do not believe that anybody should get preferential treatment merely because she happens to be a woman.

Indira Gandhi

A woman is responsible for her own freedom. She can get it without declaring war on men.

Anaïs Nin

I was horrible for many years between my marriages. I was a male basher, but every time I bashed a man it hurt rather than helped me.

Susan Jeffers

Forget the old "all men are bastards" stuff: women aren't the altruistic angels we make out to be.

Tracey Cox

It is easier to live through someone else than to become complete yourself.

Betty Friedan

THE GREAT DIVIDE

The main difference between men and women is that men are lunatics and women are idiots.

Rebecca West

There is more difference within the sexes than between them.

Ivy Compton-Burnett

But of forty-eight chromosomes only one is different: on this difference we base a complete separation of male and female, pretending as it were that all forty-eight were different.

Germaine Greer

As far as I'm concerned, being any gender is a drag.

Patti Smith

Are not sex differences exceedingly valuable, one of the resources of our human nature that every society has used but no society has yet begun to use to the full?

Margaret Mead

Men and women are like right and left hands; it doesn't make sense not to use both.

Jeannette Rankin

In men, the mind is connected to the brain. In women, the mind is connected to the heart.

Amy Tan

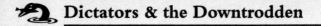

I do not believe that women are better than men. We have not wrecked railroads, nor corrupted legislature, nor done many unholy things that men have done; but then we must remember that we have not had the chance.

Jane Addams

Becoming a man is a waste of a woman.

Allison Pearson

It's Not The Men In Our Lives — It's The Life In Our Men

THE LESS-EVOLVED SPECIES

Men are the funniest things since silly putty.

Florence King

There is, of course, no reason for the existence of the male sex except that one sometimes needs help with moving the piano.

Rebecca West

My mother always told me that a man without knowledge is like a flower without scent.

Aung San Suu Kyi

Talking with a man is like trying to saddle a cow. You work like hell, but what's the point?

Gladys Upham

There's a lot of talk about functional male autism these days, mostly from me, but this must not lead us to underestimate the amount of dysfunctional male autism knocking about.

Hannah Betts

Men seem to make it their life's work to obscure what they're thinking and feeling … I can't be the only woman in the world who has to work out what her partner is feeling by a process akin to tracking spoor in a jungle.

Amanda Craig

It's Not The Men ...

The intelligent man who is proud of his intelligence is like the condemned man who is proud of his large cell.

Simone Weil

What every woman knows and no man can ever grasp is that even if he brings home everything on the list, he will still not have got the right things.

Allison Pearson

Why is psychoanalysis a lot quicker for men than for women? When it's time to go back to his childhood, he's already there.

Anonymous

They have all sunk into a realm of unreality because they cannot make babies and cannot make sense of a world in which they are so self-evidently *useless*.

Lucy Ellman

It fatigues me to death to be eternally making the agreeable to a set of men who might be all buried and nobody would miss them.

Harriette Wilson

Adam's ready acquiescence with his wife's proposal does not savour much of that superiority *in strength of mind* which is arrogated by man.

Sarah Moore Grimké

A man's mental rank may generally be determined by his estimate of woman.

Mary Cholmondeley

Man forgives woman anything save the wit to outwit him.

Minna Antrim

Don't try to teach men how to do anything in public. They can learn in private; in public they have to know.

Rita Rudner

Very marked difference between the sexes is male tendency to procrastinate doing practically everything in the world except sitting down to meals and going up to bed.

E. M. Delafield

If I. Q. was measured in inches, some of you fellas would be in trouble.

Geraldine Doyle

Don't say anything important if the sports section is within 10 feet.

Kristin van Ogtrop

THE ANIMAL ELEMENT

All men think that they're nice guys. Some of them are not. Contact me for a list of names.

Rita Rudner

The only possible purpose in a man's existence is to make one woman happy. They all seem depressingly unaware of this.

Lucy Ellman

When they stand disapprovingly in the bathroom doorway, tutting and muttering ... the implication is: men are very busy and important. They have places to go, people to see and no time to waste. Women, meanwhile, are just dawdlers.

Victoria Coren

All men are pigs, except my father and brothers.

Heidi Fleiss

The tragedy of machismo is that a man is never quite man enough.

Germaine Greer

Boys don't really "bitch" (they're too busy kicking each other's heads in). However, as they get older and find themselves in situations where kicking each other's heads isn't always a career option, men are very quick to learn the so-called "female" tricks of bitchery.

Barbara Ellen

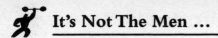

It's Not The Men ...

I like all that concerns the love adventures of these valorous knights of yore; but their deadly blows and desperate thrusts, their slashing, gashing, mashing, mangling, and hewing bore me to death. The fate of Guinevere interested me deeply, but Sir Launcelot's warlike exploits I got dreadfully weary of.

Frances Kemble

The male has a negative Midas Touch – everything he touches turns to shit.

Valerie Solanas

Bad boys are always more interesting, but I think they're something you outgrow.

Susan Sarandon

Man may be compared to a cavern. You always find damp or dirt at the bottom, or else an opening, so that in reality there is no bottom at all.

Marie Bashkirtseff

Unlike women, men menstruate by shedding other people's blood.

Lucy Ellman

When women are depressed, they eat or go shopping. Men invade another country. It's a whole different way of thinking.

Elayne Boosler

I think once you get more than three blokes together – if they're those sort of blokes – it introduces a sort of animal element into the proceedings.

Jo Brand

I like to watch men beating the crap out of each other.

Jennifer Love Hewitt

Don't look at him as a Republican but as the man I love. And, if that doesn't work, look at him as someone who can squash you.

Maria Shriver Kennedy, introducing Arnold Schwarzenegger to her family

We've had an American ethos of the male going to the frontier and leaving the confines of civilization and, in so doing, abrogating adulthood and being a perpetual adolescent.

Joyce Carol Oates

Not that life with a man is one glorious summer of song. Men get tight and are either belligerent or maudlin, they cling to their haberdashery, they repeat their old stories, they sleep with other women, they play golf or bridge or gin rummy while you languish alone, and they always want the crossword puzzle.

Ilka Chase

When I eventually met Mr Right I had no idea that his first name was Always.

Rita Rudner

Men have no humility. This makes them dangerous.

Lucy Ellman

Why is it good that there are female astronauts?
Because when the crew gets lost in space, at least the women will ask for directions.

Anonymous

Men hate to lose. I once beat my husband at tennis. I asked him, "Are we going to have sex again?" He said, "Yes, but not with each other."

Rita Rudner

There is a hidden fear that somehow, if they are only given a chance, women will suddenly do as they have been done by.

Eva Figes

CASANOVAS

Men renounce whatever they have in common with women ... and what is left, according to men, is one piece of flesh a few inches long.

Andrea Dworkin

It's Not The Men ...

Most of the world has probably always esteemed a large penis.

Camille Paglia

A woman reading *Playboy* feels a little like a Jew reading a Nazi manual.

Gloria Steinem

Male sexuality is linked with ego and women's sexuality isn't.

Jane Lapotaire

The types who make passes at girls who wear glasses – so they can see themselves in the reflection.

Stephanie Calman

A true gentleman is rare, but, fortunately, there is no crime in counterfeiting his excellences.

Mrs E. B. Duffey

Although man has learned through evolution to walk in an upright position, his eyes still swing from limb to limb.

Margaret Schooley

A gentleman is a patient wolf.

Henrietta Tiarks

One guy actually said to me, "It's a very nice dress but it would look much better on my bedroom floor."

Cameron Diaz

The male is, nonetheless, obsessed with screwing; he'll swim through a river of snot, wade nostril-deep through a mile of vomit, if he thinks there'll be a friendly pussy awaiting him.

Valerie Solanas

Alas, why will a man spend months trying to hand over his liberty to a woman – and the rest of his life trying to get it back again?

Helen Rowland

I'm not saying that all men are duplicitous bastards trying to get something for free, but you have to be careful.

Mariella Frostrup

Masculine tenderness is said to respond to tears. I do not find it so. Rather, I should say that a man's devotion fades under salt water, like a bathing-suit in the very element for which it is supposed to be adapted.

Mary Adams

Screwing, then, is a desperate compulsive attempt to prove he's not passive, not a woman; but he *is* passive and *does* want to be a woman.

Valerie Solanas

I will be the mere instrument of pleasure to no man. He must make a friend and companion of me, or he will lose me.

Harriette Wilson

Beware of loving a man. Today he says, "I love you, I need you! I shall go to the devil without you!" Tomorrow he turns to his affairs. In six months he says, "I was a fool!" Next year he says, "Who was it that drove me wild for a time last year? What was her name?"

Mary Hartwell Catherwood

As for marriage – these young men who have the world, or the better part of it – they marry where Cupidity, not Cupid, leads them.

Amelia E. Barr

I loved my father. I looked for his faithful response in the eyes of many men. None could say "forever" as he did.

Patricia Neal

No woman can devote herself exclusively to the society of men without losing some of the best and sweetest characteristics of her sex. The conversation of men of the world and men of gallantry gives insensibly a taint to the mind; the unceasing language of adulation and admiration intoxicates the head and perverts the heart.

Anna Jameson

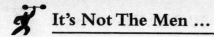

REAL MEN?

Men are brave enough to go to war, but they are not brave enough to get a bikini wax.

Rita Rudner

To be a great man, it is necessary to have done great things; but to have done great things is not always enough to become a great man.

Marie d'Agoult

It's been said of me that I get along best with men of indecision, that strong, resolute males cannot long put up with my insistence on dominating the stage, the breakfast nook or the hotel suite. These analysts have a point. I can't discipline myself to coddling my opponent.

Tallulah Bankhead

If I could have found a man to my measure, I could have put a torch to the world.

Dorothy L. Sayers

I personally would rather be teased a little and smoked over a good deal by a man whom I could look up to and be proud of than have my feet kissed all day by a Mr Smith in boots and a waistcoat, and thereby chiefly distinguished.

Elizabeth Barrett Browning

No nice men are good at getting taxis.

Katharine Whitehorn

Probably the only place where a man can feel really secure is in a maximum security prison, except for the imminent threat of release.

Germaine Greer

A civilized husband is a creature who has ceased to be a man.

Elizabeth von Arnim

I like big thighs, thundering around the playing field, the Will Carling look.

Edwina Currie

They are clearly heading towards the same tedious insecurities as women on the subject of their looks. Honestly, couldn't we have come up with something better as a compensation for millennia of oppression than making men worry they might have cellulite?

Lisa Hilton

I began to realize that the world was divided into three groups: wasters, molluscs, and builders.

Elisabeth Marbury

Why do little boys whine?
Because they are practising to be men.

Anonymous

Have we overdomesticated men, denied their natural adventurousness, tied them down to machines that are after all only glorified spindles and looms ... ?

Margaret Mead

OLDER vs YOUNGER MEN

The transition period between being a desirable, experienced older man and being a wrinkled old coot whose claw is inching toward your pert thighs only lasts about one week.

"Mom", the agony aunt for the tartcity website

Men are not as interesting at my age as women. They are playing that game you play before you die: golf.

Anita Roddick

Deep in our dark evolutionary unconscious is an obsession with reproduction, with reproductive success. That's our destiny. And that's why older men are less tormented by the loss of youth and can pass for attractive; they are still fertile.

Minette Marrin

On young men everything, like hair and teeth, is in the rightful place as opposed to being on the bedside table, dressing table or bathroom floor.

Candace Bushnell

It's Not The Men ...

One hopes they have to leave early in the morning to go to school.

Fran Lebowitz on lovers who stay overnight

Younger men are quite loyal once they've embraced the cachet of dating an older woman, especially an older woman who has spent twenty years perfecting the art of giving a blow job.

"Mom", the agony aunt for the tartcity website

I have never slept with a man older than forty-two.

Joan Collins

Nice older men have horrible young men to thank for any success they have with young women.

Barbara Ellen

A *bachelor* who hath passed forty is a *remnant*; and there is no good material left in him. His sentiments are moth-eaten and his tender speeches shop-worn. His manners shall require much basting, his morals many patches.

Helen Rowland

An old man can't do nothing for me except bring me a message from a young man.

Moms Mabley

I've dated men my age, younger than me and older. The only difference is the younger ones are quicker at taking out the garbage.

Lara Flynn Boyle

Beauty & Fashion Myths

BEAUTY IS POWER

Beauty is power.

Helena Rubinstein

A lady likes to assume that she is devastatingly attractive to even the most unattractive man whom she would happily spurn.

Ilka Chase

There is nothing on *earth* more beautiful than a beautiful woman.

Violet Keppel

I just can't understand those who have ugly people working for them, I really can't. Just call me a pathetic aesthetic.

Jade Jagger

To deny our need of beauty is to add to the ugliness of the world … We must not eradicate any quality *just* because it is associated with femininity.

Anaïs Nin

Beauty is also happiness, for which there is no prescription or explanation.

Princess Caroline of Monaco

Well, you work with what God gave you and if someone says you're pretty, you say, "Thanks very much." I guess I don't have huge artistic feminist struggles with it.

Rachel Weisz

Were my looks ever a burden? Gaad, no! I just wish I'd kissed more boys.

Deborah Harry

It is striking that the being of a woman, sited in her physical body with its different secondary sexual characteristics, has beckoned to men and women with equal lure ... Women's magazines print pictures of women on their covers; so do men's.

Marina Warner

Would you believe that I once entered a beauty contest? I must have been out of my mind. I not only came in last, I got 361 get-well cards.

Phyllis Diller

Beauty has a large prerogative.

Lady Mary Wortley Montagu

I've always been of the belief that beauty, feminism and strength go hand in hand.

Sandra Bernhard

A little beauty is what I crave; anybody can be good; wits I have myself.

Virginia Woolf

The will to be beautiful is like yeast to dough. If women are flapjacks, it is their own fault.

Mrs Tarlton in Gertrude Atherton's American Wives and English Husbands

Vanity, like murder, will out.

Hannah Cowley

Great beauty in a woman has innate sadness in it.

Marella Agnelli

Beauty is really a sense of oneself – *n'est-ce pas?*

Françoise Giraud

BRAINS & BEAUTY

I had been fed, in my youth, a lot of old wives' tales about the way men would instantly forsake a beautiful woman to flock around a brilliant one. It is but fair to say that, after getting out in the world, I had never seen this happen.

Dorothy Parker

A woman is either like a sex queen or a book-worm … I'd like to find that middle ground for a woman, also, where you can be sexy if you want to be, but you don't have to.

Suzanne Vega

It's amazing! All you have to do is look like crap on film and everyone thinks you're a brilliant actress.

Helen Mirren

Sometimes I think that no matter how hard I work it'll be attributed to how I look.

Gloria Steinem

You don't have to signal a social conscience by looking like a frump.

Jill Tweedie

Now the editors are what they should be: all chic and worldly; most of the models are out of the mind of Bram Stoker.

Dorothy Parker

The common man believes that in order to be chaste a woman must not be clever: in truth it is doing chastity too little honour to believe it can be found beautiful only by the blind.

Marie de Jars

The concept of an intelligent face being a beautiful face is a modern point of view.

Marella Agnelli

No woman could be Nietzsche or Rimbaud without ending up in a whorehouse or lobotomized.

Andrea Dworkin

WRITTEN ON THE FACE

I often stop, flabbergasted, at the sight of this incredible thing that serves me as a face.

Simone de Beauvoir

If you were to take every feature in my face, and lay them one by one on the table, there is not one single one that would bear examination. The only thing is that, put together and lighted up, they look well enough. It is homogeneous ugliness, and nothing more.

Hester Stanhope

Women are brought up to look pretty at all times. It's a legacy left to us from the days when women were women and men were gods.

Dillie Keane

In my day, the working classes didn't try to be beautiful.

Lady Diana Cooper

There never has been a really ugly heroine in fiction. Authors have started bravely out to write of an unlovely woman, but they never have had the courage to allow her to remain plain.

Edna Ferber

I don't think I'm ugly. I just think I'm overrated on the cutie-factor.

Shania Twain

While I was able to look at my face without displeasure I gave it no thought, it could look after itself.

Simone de Beauvoir

I have a lived-in face which I like very much, and as I've always said, don't f*** around with God.

Elaine Stritch

It's funny, you don't notice certain wrinkles – but you know, you can look at yourself every day but it's only once a year that you really notice a change.

Christy Turlington

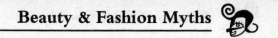

I like myself more at forty than I did at twenty, and the more I like myself the more attractive I am.

Ira von Furstenberg

SHOE-FETISHES

Why is it that all women standing by their men in public these days seem to do it in ravish-me heels?

Barbara Ellen

A well-fitted pair of shoes is equal to a facial any day.

Renee Long

I figure a little kitten heel in Hollywood is good. You might meet a producer or director …

Chloë Sevigny

I remember once I saved up to go to the chiropodist and he took one look at my feet and told me what I needed was a blacksmith.

Amanda Harlech

If high heels were so wonderful, men would be wearing them.

Sue Grafton

If the shoe fits, it's too expensive.

Adrienne E. Gusoff

Anyone with more than three hundred and sixty five pairs of shoes is a pig.

Barbara Melser Lieberman

I did not have three thousand pairs of shoes, I had one thousand and sixty.

Imelda Marcos

If God wanted us to wear flat shoes, he wouldn't have invented Manolo Blahnik.

Alexandra Shulman

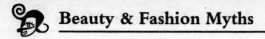

I'm going to look the way God intends … with a little help from Manolo Blahnik.

Jamie Lee Curtis

His shoes are slut pumps. You put on your Manolos and you find yourself saying "Hi, Sailor" to every man that walks by.

Joan Rivers

YOU CAN NEVER BE TOO THIN

You know you're getting fat when you step on the dog's tail and he dies.

Elayne Boosler

Make a friend of your mind. Free your mind, and your bottom will follow.

Sarah Ferguson, Duchess of York, on her slimming technique

I got out of Hastings when I was seventeen … stone.

Jo Brand

I'd never ever *ever* spoken about weight in my life, until I lost lots of it. Now I talk about it all the time. Funny that.

Rhona Cameron

I'm just short for my weight. By rights I should measure eight foot three.

Sue Margolis

A fat person is a pariah, subject to the kinds of vitriol once reserved for eighteenth-century witches.

Natalie Kusz

If the word is "infatuated", meaning that you're infatuated with someone and it's a problem because the person doesn't like you back, well, the word tells you that your problem is *in fat you ate*, meaning that you've got to eat less fat, so you'll *be* less fat, and the person you want will want you back.

Amanda Filipacchi

There is no longer a prerequisite that fat girls dress modestly, concealing their corpulence with vertical-striped, dark-coloured tents … No, if low-slung combats and spaghetti-strap vests are in, big girls want a piece of the action.

Janice Turner

I have flabby thighs, but fortunately my stomach covers them.

Joan Rivers

Give me a dozen such heart-breaks, if that would help me to lose a couple of pounds.

Colette

Most women will know how it feels to have fat days turn into fat weeks turn into fat years turn into fat lives.

Barbara Ellen

When I feel fat, I am jealous of everyone who is thin.

Paloma Picasso

For every pound I gained, I took one step backward, using flesh for padding. I bubble-wrapped my heart.

Rosie O'Donnell

If you don't show up at a party, people will assume you're fat.

Stephanie Vanderkellen

No one loves a girl who needs to have her tights taken in.

Barbara Ellen

I grew up in probably the last time and place, the 1970s working class, when it was considered perfectly normal for a woman to double her dress size between the ages of twenty and forty.

Julie Burchill

I never turned on the TV and saw Latina woman with an average body.

America Ferrara

Fat is … insidious and creepy. It is not a matter of chest-waist-hip measurement. You get fat knees, fat feet, fat in bits of you that you'd never thought of.

Hilary Mantel

There's a level of fatness – as with its far scarier, non-identical twin, self-inflicted starvation – where men, women and children have the same basic face, are literally lost inside the belly of the beast that has swallowed them.

Julie Burchill

It is understandable that we gloat over pictures of film stars, supermodels and pop singers who have visible patches of cellulite on their thighs. In these image-obsessed times, it's often the only sign of imperfection we ever see in our celebrities.

Carole Caplin

It's not my job to be thin – a fact that remains a source of endless glee to me.

Julie Burchill

BEAUTY TREATMENTS

The cosmetics industry has much to answer for. It's a multi-million-pound confidence trick based on giving women endless hope, courtesy of overpriced little pots.

Joan Collins

Make up. Meaning invent. Make up something more acceptable, because that face you have on right there will not do.

Lois Gould

I love eye makeup. Because without my eye makeup, I look like a turtle.

Phyllis Diller

Beauty doesn't come from within. It comes from putting the soft film compact rouge under the foundation.

Estée Lauder

Makeup is not beauty. When artfully applied, it merely enhances what's already there – the red paint on the fire engine.

Mae West

I believe in sheen not shine.

Estée Lauder

Nowadays there are a lot of pretty girls, cosmetics diminish the gap between beauty and mediocrity.

Liane de Pougy

If you are so worried that you have to cut your face up to make yourself happier, you're with the wrong guy.

Jerry Hall

People always ask me who does my lips. I say my mom did them. They're real.

Estella Warren

Posh is just one operation behind me.

Jordan on Victoria Beckham

I would never get a boob job. Those big-titted girls by the hotel poolsides? You just want to spit-shine them.

Juliette Lewis

I think it is much wiser to have a face-lift than to take a Valium.

Lilli Palmer

I am said to be the most "improved" woman in Europe – "improved", that is, by plastic surgery.

Ira von Furstenberg

I had a tummy tuck. This is before lipo. They didn't even know about - well, they took three pounds of fat. Actually, it was mayonnaise, mashed potatoes and gravy, out of my stomach.

Phyllis Diller

If I see a little puckering up here, I think, get some collagen, if I see a wrinkle there, I think, you'd better get some Botox. I'm like a show dog or a prize horse. You got to keep them clipped as long as they're going to be in the show.

Dolly Parton

I think Botox done by someone gifted is amazing but too many women are looking alike in a strangely spooky way.

Amanda Harlech

You seem to have developed a chronic inability to say "No" to Harrods beauty assistants. Puréed pig erections? Yes please.

Kathy Lette

When I go to bed at night, I've got so much grease on my body, I wear snow chains to hold up my gown.

Phyllis Diller

Who wants a face like Frankenstein? When I'm talking to women who've had face-lifts, I can't concentrate, because I'm so busy looking at their foreheads, how their eyebrows are sticking up over here and how their eyes do weird things when they bend down.

Jerry Hall

And the more deodorants there are in the drugstores, the worse [woman] smells in literature.

Françoise Parturier

If I could only just have back all the money I've spent on leg waxing, I could probably buy a horse.

Liz Jones

I like my bikini line, goddamn it. It's like having a little pet in my pants.

Kathy Lette

CROWNING GLORIES

It's an ill wind that blows when you leave the hairdresser.

Phyllis Diller

Women with black hair like mine were either evil queens or witches … they were always the ones who lost the man and got their just deserts in the end.

Cher

I am a big woman. I need big hair.

Aretha Franklin

Some months ago I went blonde, which is the only occasion in the whole of my political career when I have won one hundred per cent approval for something I have done.

Ann Widdecombe

People always ask me how long it takes to do my hair. I don't know, I'm never there.

Dolly Parton

When a woman ceases to alter the fashion of her hair, you guess that she has passed the crisis of her experience.

Mary Austin

I've outlived my hair.

Phyllis Diller

Gay icons usually have some tragedy in their lives, but I've only had tragic haircuts and outfits.

Kylie Minogue

COMPETITION

Some women are better than others at being female.

Jenny Eclair

It is no great wonder then, with the five caterwauling rages: femininity, vanity, age, class and cash; vying and clawing at cross purposes against each other in the beauty racket; that some of its weaker cats are scratched and mauled to carcases by the wayside.

Caitlin Thomas

Women dress alike all over the world: they dress to be annoying to other women.

Elsa Schiaparelli

Friendship is not possible between two women, one of whom is very well dressed.

Laurie Colwin

We have women in the military, but … they don't know if we can fight, if we can kill. I think we can. All the general has to do is walk over to the women and say, "You see the enemy over there? They say you look fat in those uniforms."

Elayne Boosler

Fashion is a tool … to compete in life outside the home.

Mary Quant

I don't think fashion is any more bitchy than a lot of other industries. Politics is probably far more bitchy.

Alexandra Shulman

There are people who say that beauty unadorned is adorned the most.

Fanny Douglas

For a young girl to be named "a wholesome type" is perhaps the deadliest insult of all.

Caitlin Thomas

FASHION & SEX

What woman hasn't felt that her life's journey is part meat market, part catwalk?

Barbara Ellen

All romantic novels have a preoccupation with clothes. Every sexual advance is made with clothing as an attractive barrier.

Germaine Greer

216

Fashion is about eventually being naked.

Vivienne Westwood

Isn't that the problem? That women have been swindled for centuries into substituting adornment for love, fashion (as it were) for passion?

Erica Jong

Then she tried to get me to try on a certain dress and she says, "Madam, you have got to try this dress on. It will give your husband ideas. It is so sexy." I said, "What, does a brain come with it?"

Phyllis Diller

A woman's dress should be like a barbed-wire fence: serving its purpose without obstructing the view.

Sophia Loren

Is fashionable dress part of the oppression of women, or is it a form of adult play?

Elizabeth Wilson

A woman could look like Godzilla, but if she's got blonde hair and a miniskirt, men start walking into walls.

Judy Tenuta

Pinching the bottom is sexual harassment always if the lady doesn't want it, even if she is wearing a little skirt.

Alessandra Mussolini

I see these girls in their miniskirts, their boobs hanging out and stuff. In Melbourne, the girls who wear that shit, they get beaten up. By other girls!

Holly Valance

The women who flaunt their physical assets argue that they are in control of the situation and are only doing it because they can and want to. But the, er, bottom line is still the same. Men stare at them because of what they are showing, not what they are saying.

Jane Moore

You do have to be careful not to be upstaged by your nipples.

Susan Sarandon

A full bosom is actually a millstone around a woman's neck; endears her to the men who want to make their mammet of her … Her breasts are only to be admired for as long as they show no signs of their function.

Germaine Greer

I don't know any of my friends that talk about a man's penis as the thing you shop for, but men definitely shop for breasts.

Susan Sarandon

Gut-featuring fashion is the sartorial equivalent of talking loudly, and intimately, on a mobile phone in a crowded train.

Isabel Fonseca

In the eighteenth century, things like high heels, big hoops under your skirts and elaborate wigs and hairpieces, all of these were ways of saying: I'm worth something and you people are scum.

Emma Donoghue

Interest in clothes showed a low moral nature. Whenever we were telling stories, if the story-teller said: "She was a very fashionable lady," we all knew at once that *she* was the villainess of the piece.

Gwen Raverat

Underneath your clothes, there's an endless story.

Shakira

I bought a negligé of gold lace, pink marabou, flowers, and pleated chiffon, of which Mother remarked, with the candour which has always distinguished her, that it was a tart's idea of Heaven.

Ilka Chase

Underwear is such an emotional thing.

Elle MacPherson

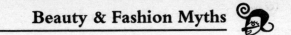

Think of the opportunities: a tight corset, causing broken ribs, fainting and an inability to breathe … and then there is the delicious job of liberating her – more titillating if still conscious: for it is a two-person job, getting in and out of a corset.

Isabel Fonseca

The Wonderbra is not a step forward for women. Nothing that hurts that much is a step forward for women.

Nora Ephron

PERSONAL STYLE

The fashionable woman wears clothes. The clothes don't wear her.

Mary Quant

The only fashion no-no is hating yourself.

Amanda Harlech

I have always said that the best clothes are invisible … they make you notice the person.

Katharine Hamnett

If fashion isn't worn by everybody, then it is only eccentricity.

Coco Chanel

I can walk into a room and make heads turn or I can walk into a room and erase myself.

Barbara Hershey

Glamour has to be sort of excessive in some way.

Alexandra Shulman

One wants to be very something, very great, very heroic; or if not that, then at least very stylish and very fashionable. It is this everlasting mediocrity that bores me.

Harriet Beecher Stowe

I curse the day that I get a best-dressed award – then I'll just ordinary.

Christina Aguilera

If one is a greyhound, why try to look like a pekingese?

Edith Sitwell

A designer is only as good as the star who wears her clothes.

Edith Head

FASHIONISTAS

Fine art at the moment is no longer particularly concerned with beauty, so you could say that fashion – which is always about a concept of beauty, whether or not everyone agrees on the concept – is more relevant, more artistic, than the garbage they put out as conceptual.

Zandra Rhodes

You can't intellectualize fashion.

Amanda Harlech

I have become anti-fashion.

Bianca Jagger

I am all for a bit of artificiality myself; which is basically what elegance is: trying to pass it off as a natural gift of God.

Caitlin Thomas

Of course, generally Italians and French have much more style.

Nancy Dell'Olio

Clothes are armour.

Donna in Melissa Bank's The Girls' Guide to Hunting and Fishing

There are two main reasons why we wear clothes. First, to hide figure flaws, of which the average person has at least seventeen. And second, to look cute, which is at least cheering.

Fran Lebowitz

I base most of my fashion taste on what doesn't itch.

Gilda Radner

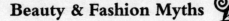

Dressing is the one art the unqualified must practise.

Elizabeth Bowen

Some women hold up dresses that are so ugly and they always say the same thing: "This looks much better on." On what? On fire?

Rita Rudner

CAN'T LIVE WITHOUT IT

Streets without shops are my personal enemies.

Misia Sert

I *can't* cure myself of liking nice clothes.

Antonia White

Fashion has a curious but compelling urgency.

Nigella Lawson

The craving for a new hat is fearful in the spring.

Katherine Mansfield

Fashion must be the intoxicating release from the banality of the world.

Diana Vreeland

There never was such a reckless Radical as Madame La Mode. She is no respecter of person.

Fanny Douglas

How many thousands trample under foot honour, ease and pleasure, in pursuit of ribands of certain colours, dabs of embroidery on their clothes, and gilt wood carved behind their coaches in a particular figure! others breaking their hearts till they are distinguished by the shape and colour of their hats; and, in general, all people earnestly seeking what they do not want while they neglect the real blessings in their possession – I mean the innocent gratification of their senses, which is all we can properly call our own.

Lady Mary Wortley Montagu

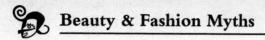

ALL THAT GLITTERS

Never trust a woman who doesn't have an instant hormonal response to diamonds.

Kate Reardon

I was at a party the other day and a nice little woman next to me said "Hello". I noticed she was wearing some rather good diamonds and then the penny dropped. It was the Queen!

Lady Diana Cooper

I do believe that a girl should pay for her own diamonds and telephone calls and never be ashamed to bargain.

Jerry Hall

I don't work out. If God had wanted us to bend over, He would have put diamonds on the floor.

Joan Rivers

Big girls need big diamonds.

Margaux Hemingway

I love costume jewellery. It is much more amusing than the real thing.

Princess Caroline of Monaco

The prime value of diamonds is that they will never make your bum look big.

Kate Reardon

I don't care for jewels. I love flowers. I like a fur coat here and there.

Ivana Trump

On Not Being A Victim

INSECURITY

Women everywhere, despite our growing power and independence, despite our longings for liberation from the way we look, are becoming more and more insecure. Our great new power, by some paradox, has coincided with an even greater new insecurity.

Minette Marrin

There is no such thing as security. There never has been. And yet we speak of security as something which people are entitled to.

Germaine Greer

Confidence is something you have to re-supply daily.

Ali MacGraw

In our darkest moments, there's always some mythical "Someone Better" lurking in the shadows, looming out of the gloom … waiting to snatch our loved one away.

Barbara Ellen

I knew I looked awful because my mother phoned and said I looked lovely.

Jo Brand, after getting a makeover on TV

I have often depended on the blindness of strangers.

Adrienne E. Gusoff

223

On Not Being A Victim

Healthy paranoia in a relationship is what makes women keep shaving their legs, and men keep changing their socks.

Barbara Ellen

It's OK when I'm playing a part, but when I have to be me it's a different thing.

Liza Minnelli

How brave, how trustful people are, to dare to go to sleep!

Jan Struther

I know full well that giddy, uprooted feeling that leaves one wondering why one is left on the earth, or why one was ever sent here.

Geraldine Jewsbury

There is no such thing as inner peace. There is only nervousness or death.

Fran Lebowitz

We mount the heights of our being, only to look down into darker colder chasms.

Margaret Fuller

BREAKING DOWN

One out of four people in this country is mentally unbalanced. Think of your three closest friends – and if they seem OK then you're the one!

Ann Landers

Neurotics are always looking for something new to overdo.

Mignon McLaughlin

It's not the tragedies that kill us, it's the messes.

Dorothy Parker

It is not good to see people who have been pretending strength all their lives lose it even for a minute.

Lillian Hellman

On Not Being A Victim

On a good day I think I'm a relatively sane person with a few frayed wires. On a bad day I think *Just lock me up.*

Rosie O'Donnell

When a person is cornered, they do unimaginable things.

Natsuo Kirino

The human heart does not stay away too long from that which hurt it most. There is a return journey to anguish that few of us are released from taking.

Lillian Smith

Neurotics dream of a good life, or a great suicide note.

Mignon McLaughlin

Do not allow yourself to cry. Tears are debilitating. They are followed by exhaustion and other extreme reactions. The only tears that should not be restrained are those of tenderness and compassion.

George Sand

I can't stand to see a man cry, that's the truth. I can't stand to see a woman cry either, but the only woman I ever really see crying to any extent is me.

Nora Ephron

This thing that we call "failure" is not the falling down, but the staying down.

Mary Pickford

SELF-LOVE/SELF-HATE

You cannot hate other people without hating yourself.

Oprah Winfrey

No person seems to me of an affectionate disposition towards others, who is not very fond of himself; yet there are some so very much attached to themselves, that they really love nothing else.

Hester Thrale

On Not Being A Victim

My boyfriend calls me "princess", but I think of myself more along the lines of "monkey" and "retard".

Alicia Silverstone

I dreaded the servants at strange houses quite as much as the hosts themselves. One could not hide from the servants; they came and looked at you in bed, and very rightly, despised your toothbrush and your underclothes.

Gwen Raverat

Self-loathing is my default setting. If all else fails, that's my reaction.

A. L. Kennedy

Women are reputed never to be disgusted. The sad fact is that they often are, but not with men; following the lead of men, they are most often disgusted with themselves.

Germaine Greer

Without being a jot wiser than my neighbours I have the peculiar misfortune to know and condemn all the wrong things I do.

Lady Mary Wortley Montagu

The biggest challenge you will have to face in your life is accepting yourself – just as you are.

Stephanie June Sorréll

Every day, I have to wake up and love myself, not in an arrogant way, but in an accepting, caring way.

Normandie Keith

To say something nice about yourself, this is the hardest thing in the world for people to do. They'd rather take their clothes off.

Nancy Friday

The man who released African killer bees in South America has apparently *forgiven* himself (hundreds of people have died).

Lucy Ellman

On Not Being A Victim

LOVING THE ENEMY

I love finding out what the new depression craze is.

Caitlin Moran

"So what?" you may think. "My obsessions might be a bit unrealistic, but at least they keep life perky. I mean, what else do I have to do with my time, take up needlepoint?"

Cynthia Heimel

Whatever foul mud might lie at the bottom of my private pond, it supports some healthy and useful growths.

Claire Rayner

It worries me that people see pain as an alien thing. There won't be any poetry written soon if everyone's on an even keel.

Susan Sarandon

Every invention, every achievement has come out of dissatisfaction, not serenity. No one ever said "Things are perfect. Let's invent fire."

Fran Lebowitz

A ship in a port is safe, but that is not what ships are built for.

Benazir Bhutto

Whenever I dwell for any length of time on my own shortcomings, they gradually begin to seem mild, harmless, rather engaging little things, not at all like the staring defects in other people's characters.

Margaret Halsey

Every middle-class person in America is on Prozac. Every poor person in America is on crack. Every middle-class person who is on Prozac has tremendous contempt for the poor person on crack.

Fran Lebowitz

I like people who stand on the edge and therefore are not sheltered.

Isabel Allende

On Not Being A Victim

Nobody can manage my worries but myself.

Elizabeth Gaskell

I am one of those people who just can't help getting a kick out of life - even when it's a kick in the teeth.

Polly Adler

I don't believe in happiness as a goal. It's a bit like the right to choose vanilla: it is just a flavour.

Tilda Swinton

It is a well known oddity that people both want to be cured, and don't want to be cured. They are afraid that, by removing their baby of wrongs, they will be left empty handed, with nothing left to nurse.

Caitlin Thomas

Happiness is not a matter of events; it depends on the tides of mind.

Alice Meynell

Nobody really cares if you're miserable, so you might as well be happy.

Cynthia Nelms

Our culture has made an enemy of the unconscious.

Doris Lessing

Freud is the father of psychoanalysis. It had no mother.

Germaine Greer

The cult of psychiatry in general has brought us nothing but trouble.

Julie Burchill

One should only see a psychiatrist out of boredom.

Muriel Spark

I literally believed all that romantic claptrap about the imperativeness of sinking to the bottom for the sake of spiritual enrichment. You may not believe I could be so fantastically daft, but there was no limit to my daftness.

Caitlin Thomas

On Not Being A Victim

I am not envious of other people's happiness. Far from it. It makes up for my want of it.

George Sand

When disappointed, I do not ask or wish consolation – I wish to know and feel my pain, to investigate its nature and its source; I will not have my thoughts diverted, or my feelings soothed.

Margaret Fuller

You can't alleviate your own suffering and you can't alleviate suffering for other people. You can't take away someone's right to suffer as much as you are.

Charlotte Rampling

EMOTIONAL PAIN

Everything suffers – man and beast, and creeping thing, and the suffering of each is to the full amount of what they can endure. I don't think there is one living who has not felt at some period that their sufferings were intolerable, too grievous to be borne.

Geraldine Jewsbury

When a writer, or an artist, has the feeling that he can't do it anymore, he descends into hell.

Edna O'Brien

There is scarcely a draught of unmingled happiness to be had in this world.

Charlotte Brontë

Don't I know that feeling … when one longs to go to a hospital and *have something cut out,* and come out minus an organ, but alive and active and like other people, instead of dragging on with this bloodless existence!!

Edith Wharton

What are nerves – are they little demons who when they find the soul forces weak rush in & strike with pitchforks all over?

Isadora Duncan

I doubt whether suffering purely mental has any good result unless it be to make us by comparison less sensitive to physical suffering.

Charlotte Brontë

What I call my pain is almost a joy seen in the wide array of the world's cruel suffering.

George Eliot

It is being unwanted that is the worst disease that any human can experience.

Mother Teresa

Does the trauma tattoo look the same on every brain?

Rosie O'Donnell

People say that time is a great healer. Which people? What are they talking about? I think some feelings you experience in your life are written in indelible ink and the best you can hope for is that they fade a little over the years.

Allison Pearson

ESCAPE FROM REALITY

Sometimes we'd rather believe the extra-somatic information (the TV weather report) rather than the somatic information (going outside and lifting our face to the sky) because that way we can pretend it really *will* be sunny tomorrow …

Nicola Griffith

Don't fight the fantasies. Enjoy them, but keep a big toe on the ground, if you can't keep your whole foot. Or two big toes.

Ruth Westheimer

Some people believe that it's a good idea to face your fears. I usually feel that it's much healthier to tie them up in a bag, drive out to the country, chuck them out your window, then drive home as fast as you can.

Ellen DeGeneres

Fearful as reality is: it is less fearful than evasions of reality.

Caitlin Thomas

Imagination and reality aren't opposites, but variations on a theme.

Lillian Stewart Carl

Of theatre, films and television, films are far and away the leaders in madness and fantasy life, wastefulness and ephemeral glory. Small wonder that so many people involved in them seem to be several sandwiches short of a picnic.

Joanna Lumley

Always facing the truth requires one of two things, absolute personal security or nothing left to lose (or at least a willingness to lose it all).

Nicola Griffith

I used to lie awake as a child and get more entertainment and terror out of blank walls and plain furniture than most children could find in a toy-store.

Charlotte Perkins Gilman

The sixties were when hallucinogenic drugs were becoming really, really big. And I don't think it's a coincidence that we had the type of shows that we had then, like *The Flying Nun*.

Ellen DeGeneres

GUILT

I had regrets by the time I was twelve.

Miranda Sawyer

Remorse presupposes enough self-forgetfulness to feel the pain of others.

Sister Helen PreJean

Make it a rule of life never to regret and never look back. Regret is an appalling waste of energy; you can't build on it; it is good only for wallowing in.

Katherine Mansfield

Brooding and agonizing over past mistakes takes energy – energy that could be used to build a decent future.

Ann Landers

When women confess, they always tell what they have not done.

Venetian proverb

I'm British born and bred, trained from toddlerdom to apologize unreservedly whenever someone else is in the wrong. "I'm sorry, but this fish is still twitching." "Sorry to be a pain, but could you move your lorry from on top of my child?" "No, I'm not going to hand over my wallet and mobile. I need them. Sorry."

Miranda Sawyer

It is hard to fight an enemy who has outposts in your head.

Sally Kempton

The ability to learn to say "no" and not feel guilty about it is the greatest success I have achieved.

Oprah Winfrey

The worst guilt is to accept an unearned guilt.

Ayn Rand

GOSSIP

The only way you can prevent people from talking about you when you leave the room is to never leave the room … Don't go to lunch. Don't go to the bathroom – wear a catheter if necessary.

Ellen DeGeneres

The human being doesn't live who won't be picked to pieces by his friends. Look for kindness in a stranger.

Ilka Chase

On Not Being A Victim

Another instance of our creative powers is our talent for slander; how ingenious are we at inventive scandal! What a formidable story can we in a moment fabricate merely from the force of a prolific imagination! How many reputations, in the fertile brain of a female, have been utterly despoiled! How industrious are we at improving a hint!

Judith Sargent Murray

Slanders are quick to produce answering echoes, if not in people's hearts at least in their mouths! No doubt this is just one of the forms of the dissatisfaction we all feel to some extent at being no more than we are … we prefer to belittle.

Simone de Beauvoir

Rumours hurt even when they're true.

Dolly Parton

Fools, fatuous individuals, tittle-tattlers, precious and conceited characters of every kind, arouse my deadly dislike.

Marie d'Agoult

The trouble with me is that I am a vindictive old shanty-Irish bitch.

Eleanor (Cissy) Patterson

Gossip is a sort of smoke that comes from the dirty tobacco-pipes of those who diffuse it; it proves nothing but the bad taste of the smoker.

George Eliot

Who is there among us whose conduct is so perfect as to close the mouth of slanderers?

Elisabetta Gonzaga

A cat fight always makes good journalism.

Erica Jong

Vendettas are food and drink for fan magazine writers and Hollywood correspondents.

Tallulah Bankhead

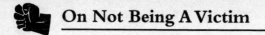

On Not Being A Victim

There are tabloids that only feed on malice.

Claire Rayner

Where journalists are concerned there is no word so derogatively stinking that it sums up the congested stink of their constipation.

Caitlin Thomas

There are some maniacs for whom no fact is really true unless it has been seen through a keyhole.

Simone de Beauvoir

Gossip is the tool of the poet, the shoptalk of the scientist and the consolation of the housewife, wit, tycoon and intellectual. It begins in the nursery and ends when speech is past.

Phyllis McGinley

I wasn't allowed to speak while my husband was alive, and since he's gone no one has been able to shut me up.

Hedda Hopper

Revenge & Other Sweet Things

TONGUE LASHINGS

When an interviewer asked Florence King "Why do you hate people?" she responded: "Who else is there to hate?"

There is a certain despairing satisfaction in finding a reason for despising everybody.

Marie Bashkirtseff

I should think you knew but little of the world, to imagine that a woman would not keep her word whenever she promised anything that was malicious.

Esther Vanhomrigh

Spite will make a woman do more than love.

Marguerite of Navarre

When females fight, the devil combs his tail.

Venetian proverb

I've always thought women were much more dangerous than men.

Tina Howe

I am the kind of woman I would run from.

Nancy Astor

Revenge & Other Sweet Things

It is generally agreed that a Bitch is aggressive and therefore unfeminine (ahem). She may be sexy, in which case she becomes a Bitch Goddess.

"Joreen": The Bitch Manifesto

And for always getting what she wants in the long run, commend me to a nasty woman.

Mrs Trenor in Edith Wharton's House of Mirth

The Devil's in her tongue, and so 'tis in most women's of her age; for when it has quitted the tail, it repairs to the upper tier.

Aphra Behn

I might take exception, if only I knew where to take it.

Judith Viorst

I succeeded by saying what everyone else is thinking.

Joan Rivers

A scratch of bitchery in a woman is a necessity if she is to be noticed.

Caitlin Thomas

Bitches are aggressive, assertive, domineering, overbearing, strong-minded, spiteful, hostile, direct, blunt, candid, obnoxious, thick-skinned, hard-headed, vicious, dogmatic, competent, competitive, pushy, loud-mouthed, independent, stubborn, demanding, manipulative, egoistic, driven, achieving, overwhelming, threatening, scary, ambitious, tough, brassy, masculine, boisterous, and turbulent. Among other things.

"Joreen": The Bitch Manifesto

I rely on my personality for birth control.

Liz Winston

A "good bitch" is like a conversational firework – you let it off, you marvel at the verbal pyrotechnics, then you let it fizzle out and forget about it.

Barbara Ellen

Sometimes the only way you can make yourself feel better is by putting other people down. And that's OK.

Ellen DeGeneres

I do like to write nasty songs. It's a useful weapon to have.

Lisa Marie Presley

I could never flatten anyone with my face. It had to be with the tongue.

Mary Hardy

In the seven years I lived in New York I managed to insult most powerful people I met.

Marge Piercy

If you have a vagina and an attitude in this town, then that's a lethal combination.

Sharon Stone

Bitching should be left to those who do it properly, who have perfected the art form over the years: women and gay men.

Barbara Ellen

If it's a woman, it's caustic; if it's a man, it's authoritative.

Barbara Walters

Just because I have my standards, people think I am a bitch.

Diana Ross

LETTING HIM/HER HAVE IT

Barbara Cartland: Baby Jane crossed with Liberace.

Julie Burchill

Mongoose-dripping cobra.

Caitlin Thomas on the mistress of her husband, Dylan

I think Mick Jagger would be astounded and amazed if he realized to how many people he is not a sex symbol.

Angie Bowie

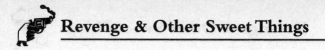

Do ya think Rod's sexy? I'm not even sure he's still alive.

Barbara Ellen

She tells enough white lies to ice a wedding cake.

Margot Asquith on Lady Desborough

Clinton isn't a leader. He's a prom king.

Fran Lebowitz on Bill Clinton

A raisin-eyed, carrot-nosed, twig-armed, straw-stuffed mannequin.

Camille Paglia on Hillary Rodham Clinton

There was no one remotely like him, except, maybe, Lucifer.

Doris Lilly on John Huston

Too chattery chittery at first go off; lean as a rake, wispy; and frittered. Some flimsy smartness and taint of the flimsy glittery literary about her: but this was partly nerves, I think; and she felt us alien and observant doubtless.

Virginia Woolf on Rose Macaulay

She is the Gagarin of gush, the Icarus of Ickiness.

Julie Burchill on journalist Justine Picardie

She was one of those strange beings who really *enjoy* discomfort, and who always remind me of the sheep in the French proverb: "*Le mouton aime la misère.*"

Gwen Raverat on Mildred Massingberd

She was divinely, hysterically, insanely malevolent.

Bette Davis on Theda Bara

Get some lessons on how to walk because you're doing a great impression of a lumbering frump.

Carol Vorderman on TV style guru Susannah Constantine

An anorexic transvestite.

Carol Vorderman on TV style guru Trinny Woodall

A carthorse in a badly fitting bin liner.

Carol Vorderman on TV style guru Susannah Constantine

She's like an apple turnover that got crushed in a grocery bag on a hot day.

Camille Paglia on Drew Barrymore

Her face was a combination of Martha Washington and the west view of Gibraltar.

Cornelia Otis Skinner on Mary, wife of Charles B. Dudley

She looks like she combs her hair with an eggbeater.

Louella Parsons on Joan Collins

She didn't wear a girdle – her ass was hanging out. She is a disgrace to the industry.

Joan Crawford on Marilyn Monroe

That's bullshit. No plane could've wiped out that son of a bitch!

Joan Blondell, on being informed that Mike Todd had died in a plane crash

If Ivana Trump outlives me, I know she'll be at my funeral because she shows up to the opening of an envelope.

Olivia Goldsmith

His dominating characteristic was that he had an unlimited love and admiration for his own person. Every day brought him the joy of rediscovering himself, and he admitted to me that his happiest moment was when he woke up in the morning and wished himself good-day.

Misia Sert on M. Périvier, editor of Le Figaro

I've never liked Mrs Currie; her Pooterish self-regard and her demon king eyebrows add up to an unfortunate package.

Julie Burchill

To call her bitchy is to over-praise her, because bitchiness entails some wit and brio, whereas Edwina just has a dull, knee-jerk contempt for everyone in her path.

Lynn Barber on Edwina Currie

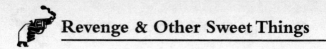

Revenge & Other Sweet Things

What's the use of having a totally gorgeous body like Victoria Principal if you've got a mind like … Victoria Principal.

Jean Kittson

Serge Gainsbourg always went out of his way to look like the before picture in a cosmetic surgeon's waiting room … a human ash-tray with duvet-sized bags between his hallucinogenic blue eyes.

Tina Brown

She has snaggle teeth, and size nine feet, and the face of a Grand National winner but once behind the camera she becomes the ultimate prairie rose.

Tina Brown on Jerry Hall

Quite frankly I've never understood what Jagger saw in that buck-toothed nag in the first place.

Camille Paglia on Jerry Hall

Her eyes have the snappy dark gaze of the kind of Parisian housewife who drives a hard bargain over an orange.

Tina Brown on Brigitte Bardot

I admire Brigitte Bardot because she has really let herself go.

Jenny Agutter

The Marquisse de Sévigné has the heart of a cucumber, fried in snow.

Ninon de Lenclos

Mrs Warren, I was constrained to think a very fine young woman, which I much regret.

Jane Austen

Saddam! Rat bastard. And I don't like France a little bit.

Chloë Sevigny

William Randolph Hearst is surely one of the most curious and complex figures in America, and many books have been written by people who hate him, and with ample reason.

Ilka Chase

240

Revenge & Other Sweet Things

Mr Cumberland's Delicacy is very troublesome, his Peevishness very teizing, & his Envy very hateful, he looks to me like a Man that had been poisoned, so sallow is his Complexion, & so sunk are his Eyes.

Hester Thrale

He looks like God after a bad day at the bookmaker.

Allison Pearson on Howard Jacobson

… a rabid Tory who thinks "blacks and gays" have it easy and who would happily give up his throne to spend the rest of his life as a ski bum if he can't blast a fox to smithereens whenever he feels the urge.

Miranda Sawyer on Prince Charles

He is not properly valued as an object. If he were in Japan, he'd be valued as some precious, lacquered treasure.

Margaret Atwood on Prince Charles

Prince Charles … doesn't even have to put his toothpaste on his toothbrush, yet looks like a cantankerous old man whose life is being ruined by urchins jamming potatoes up his drainpipe.

Caitlin Moran

Camilla could have done so much better.

India Knight on Prince Charles

He has spectacularly lost his looks. He's turned into Princess Anne.

Germaine Greer on Prince William

Just because I say that Princess Anne is a rude cow from time to time and needs her eyebrows plucking it doesn't mean I'm not devoted to the Royal Family.

Jean Rook

Maybe I channel my nasty streak into dark characters …
Apparently Meg Ryan isn't all that sweet, if you know what I mean. She might be really acting.

Anna Chancellor

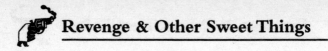

Amy's virtue was something like the nine lives of a cat.

Harriette Wilson on her sister

Dear Lady Hesketh! and how like a Naples Washball She is: so round, so sweet, so plump, so polished; so red, so white – every Quality of a Naples Wash-Ball, with more Beauty than almost any body, as much Wit as many a body … I never can find out what that Woman does to keep the people from adoring her.

Hester Thrale

She's so pure, Moses couldn't even part her knees.

Joan Rivers on Marie Osmond

She's got a great looking husband, a little boy and all the money in the world. She hasn't got the looks, but you can't have everything.

Jordan on Victoria Beckham

She was hideously boring and looked like a ferret.

Barbara Cartland on Gloria Swanson

Joan always cries a lot. Her tear ducts must be very close to her bladder.

Bette Davis on Joan Crawford

Miss Burney was much admired at Bath, the puppy Men said She had such a drooping Air, & such timid Intelligence; or a timid Air I think it was, and a drooping Intelligence.

Hester Thrale on Fanny Burney

Jon Bon Jovi is the only person I've ever interviewed who managed to make an hour feel too long.

Miranda Sawyer

He possessed also a sort of quaint, dry humour, not amounting to anything like wit; indeed, he said nothing which would bear repetition; but his affected manners and little absurdities amused for the moment.

Harriette Wilson on Beau Brummell

Revenge & Other Sweet Things

Culturally and creatively, the woman is about as interesting as overheated meringue.

Barbara Ellen on Jennifer Lopez

He resembles nothing so much as an old, sick, balding rhesus monkey.

Julie Burchill on her ex-husband, Tony Parsons

Miss Reynolds had an odd dry Manner, something between Malice and Simplicity, which was entertaining enough.

Hester Thrale

It would be hard not to torment Mrs Sweatt, who did not have a sense of humour in the way most people do not have a sense of French.

Elizabeth McCracken

I was a lady, not like that c*** Bette Davis.

Joan Crawford

[W. B. Yeats] loved great big women. He would have been mad about Vanessa Redgrave.

Rebecca West

He looks as though he's been weaned on a pickle.

Alice Roosevelt Longworth on Calvin Coolidge

Mrs Williams sets up for being a woman of great talents, tact and accomplishment – I thought there was much more noise than work.

Charlotte Brontë

Charles Powlett gave a dance on Thursday, to the great disturbance of all his neighbours, of course, who, you know, take a most lively interest in the state of his finances, and live in hopes of his soon being ruined.

Jane Austen

I'm not now an admirer of Shaw. It was a poor mind, I think. I liked his wife much better.

Rebecca West

[Somerset Maugham] couldn't write for toffee, bless his heart.

Rebecca West

As an actress her only flair is her nostrils.

Pauline Kael on Candice Bergen

As to his vulgar wife, she was ugly and unattractive enough to disgust a man with the whole fair sex, since such unfair things formed part of it.

Harriette Wilson on the wife of Doctor Tierney

She has two expressions – joy and indigestion.

Dorothy Parker on Marion Davies

A man must be a very great genius to make up for being such a loathsome human being.

Martha Gellhorn on Ernest Hemingway

His body went to his head.

Dorothy Parker on John McClain

After Wellington had left me I entirely forgot him: nay, before.

Harriette Wilson on the Duke of Wellington

Terribly hard not to dislike Evelyn Waugh.

Antonia White

He has made, I understand, a desperate conquest of Lady Caroline Lamb; but then her ladyship was never very particular you know.

Harriette Wilson on the Duke of Wellington

A monumental sexless Buddha.

Anita Loos on Gertrude Stein

Lady Hervey and Lady Bristol have quarrelled in such a polite manner that they have given one another all the titles so liberally bestowed amongst the ladies at Billingsgate.

Lady Mary Wortley Montagu

Clotheswise, he ends up looking like an IT specialist or a gay Manchester hairdresser.

Anne Robinson on Tony Blair's dress sense

Elizabeth Taylor has more chins than the Chinese telephone directory.

Joan Rivers

The stupid person's idea of a clever person.

Elizabeth Bowen on Aldous Huxley

Another meeting with that arid desert [Elinor Wylie] has sickened me. The only curiosity is – how does she do it – Francis Birrell, Aldous Huxley at her feet, and she no better than a stark staring naked maypole?

Virginia Woolf

Wellington was my constant visitor – a most unentertaining one, Heaven knows! and, in the evenings, when he wore his broad red ribbon, he looked very like a rat-catcher.

Harriette Wilson on the Duke of Wellington

If all the lies that have been uttered since the flood were put into a scale with Amy's, they would weigh as a hair in the balance.

Harriette Wilson on her sister

So you saw my Aunt! What did you think of her? Poor thing! She does not understand love. She never read "Héloïse"; but she has got a husband – such as he is.

Jane Welsh Carlyle

As far as I'm concerned, more is more. That's me. Terence Conran can go and drown himself in a coulis of is own urine if he doesn't like it.

Sue Margolis

There is often a lot of pig's ear left in these silk purses.

Elsie de Wolfe on her rich clients' lack of taste

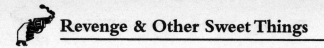

REVENGE

I think there is nothing so pleasant as revenge; I would pursue a man who had injured me to the very brink of life. I know it would be impossible for me ever to forgive him; and I would have him live only that I might have the pleasure of seeing him miserable.

Sarah Fielding

Enemies are so stimulating.

Katharine Hepburn

A lot of people ripped me off and I know who they are. I'm just glad I got there first.

Deborah Harry

I like revenge, revenge is sweet. I don't lose my temper, but I don't put a time limit on my revenge.

Jordan

I recommend obtaining some black juju voodoo power (or, hell, tinted salt will do just as well), then taking a photograph of him and placing it in an empty kitchen sink. Carefully pour a ring of your special rejection powder around the photo, then set fire to the image of your hated one while you chant something appropriate like, "I reject you, I reject you … " – or – "May your penis fall off and be eaten by wolves," – or – "May your new wife develop venereal warts," or some other appropriate curse.

"Mom", the agony aunt for the tartcity website

Even if I had known I was to go to the gallows for it, I would still have done it. This was nothing to do with revenge. I had simply learnt what it was like to have power at my fingertips – and I found I liked it.

Margaret Cook on writing her memoirs

I don't believe in revenge.

Joan Collins

I think revenge is always on yourself.

Uma Thurman

Revenge & Other Sweet Things

You can allow yourself but one sort of vengeance; it is that of doing good to such as have offended you: it is the most exquisite revenge.

The Marchioness of Lambert

No more tears now; I will think about revenge.

Mary Queen of Scots

I've never taken the time to rank my enemies. I'm afraid of hurting somebody's feelings.

Ellen DeGeneres

I think forgiveness is a lot tougher than I've had the grace to understand.

Louise Erdrich

Living hell is the best revenge.

Adrienne E. Gusoff

Animal Crackers

PETMANIA

I think all animal life, tamed or wild, the cat life, the dog life and the tiger life alike, are hidden from us and protected by darkness, they are too dark for us to read.

Stevie Smith

I like that term guardian as opposed to master or owner. It is an honour that is bestowed on some of us and we need to treat it that way.

Mary Tyler Moore

Many people will have a more enduring relationship with their pets than with their partners. Since animals can't answer back and they exchange unconditional worship for food and affection, maybe it's not surprising.

Mary Gold

A laughing human soon becomes a catnip drug dealer.

Celia Haddon

I gave my beauty and my youth to men. I am going to give my wisdom and experience to animals.

Brigitte Bardot

I don't trust anyone. That's why I surround myself with animals. They can't talk.

Jordan

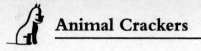

Animal Crackers

Once you've loved even one animal as a pet, you can't help but care about the welfare of all animals.

Cathy Guisewite

The journey from being harmlessly animal crackers to suffering full-blown petmania can be very short.

Mary Gold

FELINE WILES

Did St. Francis preach to the birds? Whatever for? If he really liked birds he would have done better to preach to the cats.

Rebecca West

It is better, under certain circumstances, to be a cat than to be a duchess ... no duchess of the realm ever had more faithful retainers or half so abject subjects.

Helen M. Winslow

A well-treated cat has a great desire to look handsome and groomed.

Cora Sandel

The vanity of man revolts from the serene indifference of the cat.

Agnes Repplier

Men have no understanding of cats. Cats are curvaceous and unwilling to be ordered about – men therefore have no patience with them.

Lucy Ellman

Some cats feel it is bad for discipline to let humans up on the bed.

Celia Haddon

Some people say that cats are sneaky, evil, and cruel. True, and they have many other fine qualities as well.

Missy Dizick

I am not secure enough that I can walk in the front door and have a cat stare at me and say, "Oh, it's you again."

Mary Tyler Moore

Cats don't do much except eat their dinner, show you their raw-looking bottoms and disappear for hours on end ... if a human being – a man, for example – behaved in the same way, he'd be out of the house before you could say "decree nisi".

India Knight

Have you ever had a cat in heat? They just change on you. Once she was my kitten, my adorable pet. Then, she's a hooker. I went into the bathroom one night, and she was putting on mascara, "*To*-night, *to*-night, won't be just any ... la la. Hm hm."

Ellen DeGeneres

CANINE CHARMS

I just heard on the radio yesterday that people are giving dogs Prozac. Well, there is a really good use of the gross national product. Cheering up dogs.

Fran Lebowitz

A single woman with a dog is, somehow, nowhere near as tragic as one with a cat.

India Knight

If I was a director, all of my movies would star my friends, and I would always write in a part for my dog.

Ann Patchett

There's nothing like having a dog for getting the low-down on what's happening locally. Dog people are terrible gossips and I do love gossip.

Jenny Eclair

A dog connects you to the world in a way that nothing else can. "Oh, a boxer!! I had a boxer when I was growing up!!" You can be walking down the street with your mother, and no one stops and says, "Oh, a mother! I had a mother when I was growing up!"

Elayne Boosler

In the unlikely event of the monarchy's abolition, the corgis probably wouldn't find the transition too traumatic; after all, they're not the only pets in the country to be treated like royalty.

Justine Hankins

Some people have *surprise* birthday parties for their dogs. That's just a waste, because any party would be a surprise to a dog.

Ellen DeGeneres

Dogs have better manners than the English – at least they greet each other.

Katharine Hamnett

Ever consider what dogs must think of us? I mean, here we come back from a grocery store with the most amazing haul – chicken, pork, half a cow. They must think we're the greatest hunters on earth!

Anne Tyler

Don't accept your dog's admiration as conclusive evidence that you are wonderful.

Ann Landers

Half the horrors of illness cease when one has a book or a dog or a cup of one's own at hand.

Virginia Woolf

I'm smarter than my dogs. Well, smarter than one of my dogs.

Ellen DeGeneres

ANIMAL RIGHTS

In cities, people want other people. The real trick will be learning to share the changing urban scene with our newest and most determined immigrants, the ones with wings. Or scales. Or paws.

Anne Matthews

After all, humans are animals, too.

Rita Mae Brown

I don't have a switch in my head to turn off the suffering of animals.

Linda Blair

I'm for guns. I think we should give them to everybody. Especially ducks. How can you call hunting a sport when only one side has a chance of winning?

Elayne Boosler

Good food is a celebration of life ... That is why I don't eat flesh. I see no need for killing.

Anna Thomas

Grandmother once took her umbrella to a man who was beating a horse and when she was through with him, he was glad to be turned over to the police.

Ilka Chase

If I'm facing a theatre filled with people in fur coats, I open with the anti fur material. No sense preaching to the converted. Which is why I always get paid before the show.

Elayne Boosler

When I see people wearing fur, I'm not sure if I should be chucking something at them or saying something. There's no good reason for wearing fur. And it even looks crap.

Sophie Ellis Bextor

These are the two biggest crimes you can commit in this country. Smoking while wearing a fur coat – my image of someone doing this is Carole Lombard. Everyone else's image seems to be Adolph Eichmann.

Fran Lebowitz

Rodents are nocturnal, they're not like us at all, the reason why they use them is because they're easy to handle, they multiply fast, they're small. That's not science.

Grace Slick

Home Is Where The Heartache Is

HOUSEWORK CAN'T KILL YOU, BUT ...

Housework can't kill you, but why take a chance?

Phyllis Diller

When it comes to housework the one thing no book of household management can ever tell you is how to begin. Or maybe, I mean why.

Katharine Whitehorn

The two extremes of perfectionism in American cultural life ... Martha Stewart, and the Earth Mother who does everything more naturally than you.

Lynne Siprelle

I remember growing up in the '70s that the worst thing you could say about someone was that they were going to grow up to be a housewife. Like, "You scum."

Ariel Gore

Don't let the number of women in the work force trick you – there are still lots of magazines devoted almost exclusively to making perfect casseroles and turning various things into tents.

Nora Ephron

Domestic Goddesses who say they get high on housework have obviously been inhaling too much cleaning fluid.

Kathy Lette

It's a small world … But not if you have to clean it.

Anonymous

I was a chambermaid once as a student and I was so bad at it I got sacked. Apparently my bathroom skills needed remedial training.

Emma Donoghue

I do like Hoovering, though. I also like rubber gloves. It's not a fetish thing, it's more like wearing red shoes.

Zoë Ball

I'm not going to vacuum 'til Sears makes one you can ride on.

Roseanne Barr

If my furniture ever annoyed me by wanting to be dusted when I wanted to be doing something else, and there was no one to do the dusting for me, I should cast it all into the nearest bonfire and sit and warm my toes at the flames with great contentment.

Elizabeth von Arnim

I could be Martha Stewart too if I had staff.

Lynne Siprelle

Rest assured that as long as I live I will never deteriorate to the level of a housefleur, a nice domestic creature who orders lunch and keeps accounts, a mere instrument of procreation, a matron, a housekeeper – pah!

Violet Keppel

There is something about filling out printed forms which arouses lawless impulses in me … Today, when one of my blanks said OCCUPATION, I wrote … *parasite* … This made the official relax a little and he himself put *housewife* in what space was left. "Be a prince," I said. "Make it *typhoid-carrier*."

Margaret Halsey

Scrubbing … doesn't seem to me to be a human occupation at all. I'd rather keep the floor moist and grow a crop of grass on it.

Katherine Mansfield

Home Is Where The Heartache Is

My second favourite household chore is ironing. My first being hitting my head on the top bunk bed until I faint.

Erma Bombeck

I buried a lot of my ironing in the back yard.

Phyllis Diller

I make no secret of the fact that I would rather lie on a sofa than sweep beneath it. But you have to be efficient if you're going to be lazy.

Shirley Conran

Housework is work directly opposed to the possibility of human self-actualization.

Ann Oakley

The labour of women in the house, certainly, enables men to produce more wealth than they otherwise could; and in this way women are economic factors in society. But so are horses …

Charlotte Perkins Gilman

He's not even slightly housetrained, and believe me I've made many attempts. He says things like, "when I feel the urge to be useful you'll be the first to know."

Pamela Stephenson on her husband, Billy Connolly

You must be useless when you get home to your husband. Whatever happened in the last century, the guy's role is to care for you, so let him do it. Be a princess from the beginning.

Anne Robinson

A woman fit to be a man's wife is too good to be his servant.

Dorothy Leigh

Dirty dishes, dirty diapers, dusty floor, unwashed bodies, smeared woodwork, vomit, soiled clothes and dandruff are quite simply the effects of Eve's fall and must be accepted as such.

Solange Herz

I feel very moral to-day, having done a big wash alone, baked, swept the house, picked the hops, got dinner, and written a chapter in "Moods".

Louisa May Alcott

It comes down to this. Someone must wash the dishes. Now, would you expect man, man made in the image of God, to roll up his sleeves and wash the dishes? Why, it would be blasphemy. I know that I am but a rib and so I wash the dishes. Or I hire another rib to do it for me, which amounts to the same thing.

Marie Jenney Howe

The fantasy that equates time at home with so-called free time is a strictly masculine delusion.

Susan Maushart

Housekeeping ain't no joke.

Louisa May Alcott

Men's contributions to domestic labour, by contrast, are in many households still greeted with awe and ceremony, as befits an occasion.

Susan Maushart

What if a man tries to be part of the home - will the woman let him? I answer yes. Because then he becomes one of the children.

Marguerite Duras

After all, it's not as if there is some "instinct to vacuum" which women have and men lack.

Susan Maushart

INTERIOR DECORATING

For a lot of women their house is their art form.

Alison Lurie

The dead hand of good taste has commenced its last great attempt to buy up every soul on the planet.

Tilda Swinton

Home Is Where The Heartache Is

A woman's quest in life should be to find the perfect apartment.

Fran Lebowitz

To be a feminist and a subscriber to *Martha Stewart Living*, then, can be a complicated proposition. One feels the need to qualify the interest in domesticity with a twist on the *Playboy* reader's insistence that he only buys the magazines for the articles.

Sarah A. Leavitt

Home wasn't built in a day.

Jane Sherwood Ace

In furnishing one's place of residence … one is invariably drawn to such fixtures as Cocteau drawings, Ming vases, and Aubusson rugs. Comfort is, of course, assured by the ability to possess these objects. Usefulness is something best left to those trained in such matters.

Fran Lebowitz

Just as a cigar is never really just a cigar, a living room can never be just a living room.

Sarah A. Leavitt

To be truly happy in a house, to really know it and own it, you have to work on it from top to bottom.

Elizabeth Jane Howard

The starring role of Housewife – a woman who married a house.

Maeve Binchy

This is a vast house and a small monkey could be put away anywhere. I feel it to be a lost opportunity.

Vanessa Bell

All I need is room enough to lay a hat and a few friends.

Dorothy Parker

I had a villa built for me, found it rather amusing, and thereafter building became my hobby. I invented a style which I found wonderfully suitable to the Mediterranean climate, and soon houses grew around me like mushrooms.

Misia Sert

I have never indulged in the snobbery of living in a house far from the shopping centre.

Misia Sert

Some women can never make the place where they live look like a home. Others, even if they only spend a night in a room give it a belonging atmosphere.

Noel Streatfield

I believe in plenty of optimism and white paint.

Elsie de Woolf

People go to the gallows still thinking about white paint.

Min Hogg

People think, oh, she lives in this fabulous place, but it's the same old place. It started out like a farm, it got to be a farmette, then it got to be an estatelet. I built a wall; it helped a lot.

Martha Stewart

In New York City, one suicide in ten is attributed to a lack of storage space.

Judith Stone

DOMESTIC BLISS

To create harmony in the home is the woman's right and duty.

Princess Grace of Monaco

Home is a place not only of strong affections, but of entire unreserve; it is life's undress rehearsal, its backroom, its dressing room.

Harriet Beecher Stowe

Home as it turns out is a place to which one properly belongs, in which one's affections centre, or where one finds refuge, rest or satisfaction.

Carrie Fisher

"Home" is any four walls that enclose the right person.

Helen Rowland

Home Is Where The Heartache Is

Homesickness seems to me one of the most terrible maladies, and one which you do not necessarily outgrow with age. It lies in wait like a recurrent illness, and sometimes, quite unexpectedly, the old familiar pain will surge over you.

Ilka Chase

In the late '60s, '70s, women went to work, they went crazy. They thought the workplace was much more exciting than the home. They thought the family could wait. And you know what? The family can't wait.

Martha Stewart

A sparkling house is a fine thing if the children aren't robbed of their lustre in keeping it that way.

Marcelene Cox

Try to put in the hearts of your children a love for home. So much sin could be avoided if people really loved their homes.

Mother Teresa

A happy home is the best and surest safeguard against all evil; and where home is not happy, there the devil may freely enter and find his hands full.

Marie Corelli

I'm sure that the upper classes have such a reputation for bed-hopping because vigorous sex was the only way you could keep warm in large country houses.

Jilly Cooper

Family to me is closely associated, with, like, strapping 500-pound bricks to my feet and jumping in the water.

Drew Barrymore

People are unwilling to notice that no one has a home anymore. The middle class has no motherhood in it. The lower class has no fatherhood in it. The upper class has neither.

Fran Lebowitz

MOTHER CHRISTMAS

Before I give myself over to Christmas good will, I am making a list of the people whom I would like to murder. Every day I collect a few more, and I am knitting their descriptions into a huge purple stocking. I do not know any of their names.

Janet Hills

The problem with Christmas – rather like having a baby – is that it occurs infrequently enough for us to be able each time to blot out the horrors of the previous one.

Jilly Cooper

Christmas Day itself was organized by Lady Bobbin with the thoroughness and attention to detail of a general leading his army into battle. Not one moment of its enjoyment was left to chance or to the ingenuity of her guests; these received on Christmas Eve their marching orders, orders which must be obeyed to the letter on pain of death.

Nancy Mitford

Did I tell you about my Blasphemous Dream? … I dreamt I was hostess – or perhaps merely housekeeper – at the Last Supper, and after a period of increased, repressed housewifely irritation, felt obliged to say to the assembled Binjers: "Please, *please,* don't fill up on all that Bread and Wine – there's a good roast shoulder of mutton coming … "

Stella Benson

Sometimes think that the roles of housewife and practising Christian are quite incompatible.

Rosamund Dashwood

What was in it for any woman? Women, who rarely earned any money, suddenly became a conduit for cash.

Maeve in Clare Boylan's The Alternative Christmas

Home Is Where The Heartache Is

Christmas is the Devil's own feast not the other way round, as generally supposed. Once when our singing mistress asked me why I hung up my stocking on Christmas Eve, I said it was to celebrate the crucifixion.

Virginia Woolf

Looking around on the tired, worn, nervous, querulous faces in the crowds that fill the streets and shops at Christmas-time – hearing the endless complaints, the new diseases, the troubles, real and fancied, of each person who can manage to detain a friend for five minutes' hurried and morbid conversation – reading the delectable details of suicide, murder, mania and misadventure preciously garnered up as gems of literature for the million by the halfpenny press – one may reasonably wonder whether England was ever in truth really "merrie," as recorded.

Marie Corelli

I forget the derivation of Boxing Day, but the feeling of wanting to invite your loved ones outside one at a time and punch them in the face, does that come into it somewhere?

Allison Pearson

New Year's Eve is a great deal more fun in theory than in practice ... New Year's Eve has become the national quintessential Saturday night, set aside as a social occasion with built-in disappointments for everyone. There is nothing like an officially designated time of glamour and excitement for producing mass discontent and depression.

Judith Martin as "Miss Manners"

NATURE & THE ENVIRONMENT

Even though we're so high-tech, we don't want to grow so fast and so far that we forget that we come from the dirt and the land.

Dolly Parton

Those who love Nature truly never quite lose their childlike impressions of her.

Beatrice Harraden

I think it pisses God off if you walk by the colour purple in a field somewhere and don't notice it.

Celie in Alice Walker's The Colour Purple

Nature in America has always been suspect, on the defensive, cannibalized by progress. In America, every specimen becomes a relic.

Susan Sontag

The long sight lines, that long shoot of the eye to a distant horizon for some reason frees thoughts and images for me more than anywhere else. I love northern New England, but the trees get in the way of thinking for me.

E. Annie Proulx

Give me town or country *en grand!* Solitude or the best society; but I abhor little sixpenny assembly-places.

Harriette Wilson

The Country is like a good woman abandoned for a bad woman: who is the Town.

Caitlin Thomas

If I spend two weeks in the country, I feel like I'm living in New Zealand – having a lovely time, but completely cut off from where things are happening.

India Knight

Environmentalists have long been fond of saying that the sun is the only safe nuclear reactor, situated as it is some ninety-three million miles away.

Stephanie Mills

We are citizens of Earth, her joyriders and her caretakers, who would do well to work on her problems together.

Diane Ackerman

What have we done to the earth in the pursuit of money?

Jane Lapotaire

Home Is Where The Heartache Is

We are living beyond our means. As a people we have developed a life-style that is draining the earth of its priceless and irreplaceable resources without regard for the future of our children and people all around the world.

Margaret Mead

I go down through the garden and prune, and pick, and do all those things, I keep grounded, and by keeping grounded you can then see very clearly what's happened to you.

Martha Stewart

Nature is the wisest, the only infallible teacher, and her lore is inexhaustible. Books are but her interpreters, and, though valuable aids when she is silent, are never to be preferred to her lessons of wisdom.

Harriet Martineau

One should not say: the universe, for how is it possible to gather into one concept what cannot be measured?

Edith Södergran

Travels & Adventures

THE ART OF TRAVEL

Who dies in the same house in which they were born? There must be a nomad hiding in us all: he's not our best friend.

Fay Weldon

The best travel is that which one can take by one's own fireside, in memory or imagination.

George Eliot

The great and recurrent question about abroad is, is it worth getting there?

Rose Macaulay

Perhaps, however, it may be a satisfaction to some folks to spend their surplus cash in "furrin parts" rather than at home? If this should be the case, it will be an equal satisfaction to me to politely intimate that I consider such persons unworthy of their own matchless country. The much abused "English climate" is good enough for anybody.

Marie Corelli

A sense of place is also a sense of self.

Anne Matthews

"Abroad," that large home of ruined reputations.

George Eliot

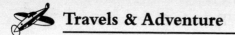

Most expeditions and interactions are suburb-to-suburb; you create your own metropolis, measuring distance in travel time, not in miles from some distinctive feature like Times Square or Chicago's Loop. Everyone's galactic-city map is different – urbanism à la carte.

Anne Matthews

Travel is the frivolous part of serious lives, and the serious part of frivolous ones.

Anne Sophie Swetchine

My body fights travel, sends up the weapons of a homeless person, the boundaries thinly drawn, the body with its own knowledge, disorientations, defences …

Lorrie Moore

Much though I love my own sex, my gorge heaves at the travelling female.

Virginia Woolf

I must confess I have no sympathy with the restless, nervous swarms of semi-lunatics ever "on the go" in search of "change"; who turn their backs on Imperial Britain at the first breath of winter.

Marie Corelli

It seems to me that the perception of innocence prepares us for the reception of education. So it is not surprising that I continue to find myself most at home in places that I do not belong, places that feel brand new yet intimate and filled with potential godshots.

Elaine Dundy

Certainly, travel is more than the seeing of sights; it is a change that goes on, deep and permanent, in the ideas of living.

Miriam Beard

I am in love with travelling and with books: also with travel books, books to read while travelling and books as secret personal journeys.

Joanna Lumley

Personally, I have always found daily routine more tiring than travel.

Elizabeth Forsythe Hailey

Security is mostly a superstition. It does not exist in nature, nor do the children of men as a whole experience it. Avoiding danger is no safer in the long run than outright exposure. Life is either a daring adventure, or nothing.

Helen Keller

There is a conservative in every adventurer. To create his image, to project his legend into the future, the adventurer needs a stable society.

Simone de Beauvoir

[Travel seems] not just a way of having a good time, but something that every self-respecting citizen ought to undertake, like a high-fibre diet, say, or a deodorant.

Jan Morris

There is a science to travel which is perfected only with time and experience.

Alice-Leone Moats

I have, thanks to my travels, added to my stock all the superstitions of other countries. I know them all now, and in any critical moment of my life, they all rise up in armed legions for or against me.

Sarah Bernhardt

It is somehow reassuring to discover that the word "travel" is derived from "travail," denoting the pains of childbirth.

Jessica Mitford

Whenever I prepare for a journey I prepare as though for death.

Katherine Mansfield

Getting all wrought up seldom helps except, of course, in Latin countries.

Alice-Leone Moats

The tourist may complain of other tourists, but he would be lost without them.

Agnes Repplier

On a plane you can pick up more and better people than on any other public conveyance since the stagecoach.

Anita Loos

Travel, instead of broadening the mind, often merely lengthens the conversation.

Elizabeth Drew

Humour is the first of the gifts to perish in a foreign tongue.

Virginia Woolf

I never leave a country without buying something either fragile, heavy or dangerous to transport, and sometimes, it's all three.

Tama Janowitz

White is glamorous because it's impractical or really hard to maintain. People who travel are glamorous because they're not doing the same thing, they're not doing the everyday.

Alexandra Schulman

Danger gives a *haut goût* to every thing.

Lady Mary Wortley Montagu

Never decline excitement.

Cynthia Heimel

TRAINS

The trains are much loved by me; their language is companionable, familiar, pregnant with interest and surprises: triumphant masculine crescendos, gently lamenting diminuendos, hoarse throaty chucklings, indignant hoots, unbridled snorts and explosions, exhausted sighs and snuffles.

Rosamund Lehmann

A private railroad car is not an acquired taste. One takes to it immediately.

Eleanor Robson Belmont

The sordid and heart-rending sadness of railway stations! A sadness that belongs to poverty, a grimy sadness, composed of inhaled soot and tears, of peeling posters and deadly draughts.

Misia Sert

Alone on a train, I feel my life could go in any direction.

Elizabeth Forsythe Hailey

Some day I should like to have a heart-to-heart talk with the pixies who arrange European train schedules.

Ilka Chase

AMERICA

Americans are very friendly and very suspicious, that is what Americans are and that is what always upsets the foreigner.

Gertrude Stein

When I got to America I found myself in a completely masculine culture, but where men were afraid of women.

Anaïs Nin

I think the climate is largely responsible for some that is wacky and much that is shoddy in southern California. They say you go to hell in the tropics.

Ilka Chase

All creative people should be required to leave California for three months every year.

Gloria Swanson

Unfortunately, there's a big anti-intellectual strain in the American south, and there always has been. We're not big on thought.

Donna Tartt

The character of the American literature is, generally speaking, pretty justly appreciated in Europe. The immense exhalation of periodical trash, which penetrates into every cot and corner of the country, and which is greedily sucked in by all ranks, is unquestionably one great cause of its inferiority.

Frances Trollope

All the American women had purple noses and grey lips and their faces were chalk white from terrible powder. I recognized that the United States could be my life's work.

Helena Rubinstein

America is not a melting pot. It is a sizzling cauldron.

Barbara Mikulski

Thank God we're living in a country where the sky's the limit, the stores are open late and you can shop in bed thanks to television.

Joan Rivers

In Tulsa, restaurants have signs that say, "Sorry, we're open."

Roseanne Barr

NEW YORK, NEW YORK

It is ridiculous to set a detective story in New York City. New York City is itself a detective story.

Agatha Christie

As only New Yorkers know, if you can get through the twilight, you'll live through the night.

Dorothy Parker

I had to move to New York for health reasons. I'm very paranoid and New York is the only place where my fears are justified.

Anita Wise

New York: The only city where people make radio requests like, "This is for Tina – I'm sorry I stabbed you."

Carol Leifer

Even thin people look fat there.

Roseanne Barr

I don't think New York is any longer a place to make things. I think it's just a place to sell them.

Fran Lebowitz

New York is the most exciting city in the world in which to know success.

Janet Baker

I don't see how people ever have money enough to live here.

Dorothy Gish

New York is largely made up of aggressively private space; it's the most regulated, subdivided, profit-driven landscape in history.

Anne Matthews

When you leave New York, you are astonished at how clean the rest of the world is. Clean is not enough.

Fran Lebowitz

CANADA

For some reason, a glaze passes over people's faces when you say "Canada".

Sondra Gottlieb

Canadians are Americans with no Disneyland.

Margaret Mahy

Canada was built on dead beavers.

Margaret Atwood

Canadians are cold so much of the time that many of them leave instructions to be cremated.

Cynthia Nelms

ENGLAND

When it's three o'clock in New York, it's still 1938 in London.

Bette Midler

The difference is prodigious between England and perhaps all the continental nations in this respect of social conventionality.

Elizabeth Barrett Browning

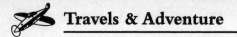

There are worse places than Hastings … Beirut and Sarajevo spring to mind.

Jo Brand

This Englishwoman is so refined
She has no bosom and no behind.

Stevie Smith

There was nothing in the world so restful as a really good English colonel.

Jan Struther

English men. Charm the knickers off you with their mellow vowels and frivolous verbiage, and then, once they'd got them off, panic and run.

Margaret Atwood

This beautiful England is always the same – an endless chain of perfections which appeal to the reason but leave the imagination untouched. For a couple of months you may be enraptured by the country, for everything seems at first so beautiful, and then so extraordinary, that one's sense of admiration is constantly excited; but when one has seen everything, and grown tired of admiring, one wishes to feel, and England is not the country of emotions.

Dorothea Christorovna Benckendorff, Princess Lieven

It is possible to have too much Natural History in a bed.

Beatrix Potter, on finding bed bugs in her Torquay hotel room

I expected England to be green, but I had not visualized anything so juicily and fervently green as it turned out to be.

Margaret Halsey

I should like to put a great notice over England – *closed* during the winter months.

Katherine Mansfield

We are as much blinded in England by politics and views of interest as we are by mists and fogs, and 'tis necessary to have a very uncommon constitution not to be tainted with the distempers of our climate. I confess myself very much infected with epidemical dullness.

Lady Mary Wortley Montagu

I'd never heard of sticking gerbils up your ass before I came here.

Lucy Ellman

SCOTLAND

The best way to see Scotland is to take the train to Edinburgh, hire a clapped-out Cortina and a clan chieftain's son to drive it. With this basic equipment, you can dial your way through *Debrett's*, soliciting beds for the night in historic houses.

Tina Brown

There is no place like Scotland to bring roses to a woman's cheeks. Probably the excess of moisture is good for the skin, and it *does* rain there continually.

Lillie Langtry

IRELAND

In some parts of Ireland the sleep which knows no waking is always followed by a wake which knows no sleeping.

Mary Wilson Little

FRANCE

A Frenchman is a German with good food.

Fran Lebowitz

And the French, of course, are utterly *outré*. Where else could you find a toy poodle in full fig of plaid tam o'shanter and manicured toenails sharing a table with its mistress at a top restaurant?

Mary Gold

The French are foppish, and will be foppish, no Philosophy can cure them.

Hester Thrale

I have yet to meet a Frenchman who does not consider himself my superior.

Elizabeth Forsythe Hailey

I like Frenchmen very much, because even when they insult you they do it so nicely.

Josephine Baker

It is hard, galumphing along through a sea of French women who have exquisite shoes and haircuts, overbites unruined by orthodontia, faces unbedecked by optometry, a great, nearsighted, chomping faith in their own beauty that makes them perhaps seem prettier than they are.

Lorrie Moore

Let me assure you on this front: fantasies about French women are far superior to the reality of French women.

"Mom", the agony aunt for the tartcity website

Veneration of woman is a national trait, that is, provided woman stays in her proper environment – the *foyer*, the salon, the restaurant, always, of course, with a male escort and preferably engaged in that agreeable pastime known as *le flirting*.

Cornelia Otis Skinner

The South of France is fever to the feverish.

Katherine Mansfield

Friendship in France [is] as impossible to be attained as orange trees on the mountains of Scotland.

Lady Mary Wortley Montagu

They tell me Saint-Tropez is uninhabitable this year. You only find people whose photograph appears in *Vogue*.

Colette

PARIS

Paris is a hostile brilliant alien city.

Virginia Woolf

The tragedy is that such a city should have become only a beautiful shell, enclosing a corrupt and cynical body politic. Through her lovely streets walk the men who betrayed her.

Ilka Chase

Being broke in London is miserable, but being broke in Paris is quite nice.

Kristin Scott Thomas

Paris is a great beauty. As such it possesses all the qualities one finds in any other great beauty: chic, sexiness, grandeur, arrogance, and the absolute inability and refusal to listen to reason.

Fran Lebowitz

ITALY

There are some places we remember with pleasure, because we have been happy there; others, because endeared to us as the residence of friends. We love our country because it is *our country;* our home because it is *home:* London or Paris we may prefer, as comprehending in themselves, all the intellectual pleasures, and luxuries of life: but, dear Italy! – we love it, simply for its own sake.

Anna Jameson

Travelling is the ruin of all happiness! There's no looking at a building after seeing Italy.

Fanny Burney

Had I never visited Italy I think I should never have understood the word *picturesque* … Civilization, cleanliness, and comfort, are excellent things, but they are sworn enemies to the picturesque.

Anna Jameson

I only speak fashion Italian – "molto bene collezione Signor Armani", "magnifico, Donatella!", "Ciao, bella, mwah-mwah Domenico Dolce e Stefano Gabbana … "

Kathryn Flett

At home a forty-five-year-old widow is considered old; in Italy she is merely regarded as ripe.

Elizabeth Forsythe Hailey

One assumes that foreign ladies, English and Americans particularly, because they are tremulous, neurotic bags of bone reduced by sexual malnutrition, find all Italians irresistible.

Kate Simon

Romans are the Rolls-Royce of men.

Ivana Trump

Rome took all the vanity out of me; for after seeing the wonders there, I felt too insignificant to live, and gave up all my foolish hopes in despair.

Amy in Louisa May Alcott's Little Women

The Romans did plenty that wasn't worth imitating, so forget about that phrase.

Ann Landers

A *Napoletano* can pirate your purse while exalting your beauty or the fine cut of your coat. He is sincere, open-hearted, even, in the fulfilment of all his missions. *Napoli* is the brigand lover whose embrace, for all the world, one would not have, for a night, forsaken.

Marlena de Blasi

An English child at Venice, on seeing the Place St. Mark for the first time, said, "Pray, Mamma, are people allowed to see this every day, or only on holidays?"

Anne Matthews

She deserves something better than to be kept as an antiquated toy, for the amusement of travelling ladies and gentlemen, in the rococo line of research.

Frances Trollope on Venice

It fulfils all the exigencies of romance; it is the only thing that has never disappointed me.

Isabel Burton on Venice

It is better to go there with a lover, because otherwise frustrations may set in.

Ilka Chase on Venice

EUROPE

What is there about travelling in Europe that makes one view one's own life as part of history?

Elizabeth Forsythe Hailey

Every nation in Europe and Asia has simultaneously denied and boasted that it had a national character.

Ruth Benedict

I always feel you can do Europe in a wheelchair.

Erma Bombeck

I have heard somewhere that if you strip a Spaniard of all his good qualities he becomes a Portuguese.

Hester Thrale

Russia's a little bit like a critically ill patient. You have to get up every day and take the pulse and hope that nothing catastrophic happened the night before.

Condoleezza Rice

Germans possess too much pedantic thoroughness and too little intellectual grace; when they know something, immediately a heavy dissertation with a bagful of citations results instead of a light sketch.

Rosa Luxemburg

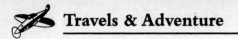 **Travels & Adventure**

Switzerland, which I have always managed to avoid, is the very devil I knew it would be. I mean the people are so UGLY; they are simply hideous. They have no shape. All the women have pear shaped derrières, ugly heads, awful feet.

Katherine Mansfield

"Anyone wishing to pick her nose should do so now," said Eloïse's father as the car entered another tunnel on their trip through Switzerland.

Lucy Ellman

In Spain I hear so much noise from my window that I can't stand it. In Switzerland it's the lack of noise that drives me crazy.

Geraldine Chaplin

Since my arrival I have been able to breathe again at my ease, in Geneva I felt like a carp on the grass.

Marie d'Agoult

The Tide Will Turn

ADVERSITY

When you get into a tight place and everything goes against you until it seems that you cannot hold on for a minute longer, never give up then, for that is just the place and time that the tide will turn.

Harriet Beecher Stowe

Sometimes it is enough to admit your own powerlessness. Enough to just be like the bulb in the deep earth. No one has asked you to believe that the sun will come again. And it doesn't matter – it will come anyway.

Stephanie June Sorréll

Let go of the things that can't possibly matter to you, and you'll always have room for the better things that come along.

Mae West

To gain that which is worth having, it may be necessary to lose everything else.

Bernadette Devlin

It is enough to stand without hope and honour your emptiness with dignity.

Stephanie June Sorréll

I've learnt to make disappointment my friend because if you do, it allows different opportunities to arise … I still want to be surprising people when I'm in my fifties.

Rachel Griffiths

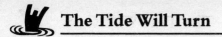
I have always taken my failures well; they were nothing but shots off target, never obstacles in my path.

Simone de Beauvoir

I don't believe in failure. It is not failure if you enjoyed the process.

Oprah Winfrey

If we had no winter, the spring would not be so pleasant; if we did not sometimes taste of adversity, prosperity would not be so welcome.

Anne Bradstreet

Never mind about present affliction – any moment may be the next.

Jacqueline du Pré

I feel I have been allowed to survive in order to carry a message about survival.

Susan Vreeland

WOMEN'S ILLS

Even if I read about a disease and it says, "This disease is present only in seventy-year-old Asian men," I feel, Oh! I could be the first white woman to have this disease.

Fran Lebowitz

Hysteria comes from the Greek word for the womb, and wombs are now seen as optional extras to the female, not the root of their being, as once they were.

Fay Weldon

Hysteria, like everything else, comes with practice.

Caitlin Thomas

Women complain about premenstrual syndrome, but I think of it as the only time of the month that I can be myself.

Roseanne Barr

One would suppose in reading them that women possess but one class of physical organs, and that these are always diseased.

Mary Ashton Livermore on books written by men physicians

I only use Doctor Donoghue at the dentist because I went in once feeling particularly disempowered, as you do, you know?

Emma Donoghue

A male gynaecologist is like an auto mechanic who never owned a car.

Carrie Snow

I love to go to the doctor. Where else would a man look at me and say, "Take off your clothes?"

Phyllis Diller

A woman's body works as if it knew something she didn't, and does not have her best interests at heart. If you need to look your best it will deliver you a pimple; if you don't want it to, your period will start early; if you want a baby badly your body refuses to give you one; if you are content in your life, lo, you are pregnant.

Fay Weldon

When I awoke from the operation, a young nurse looked at my chart and remarked coldly: "Had yourself spayed, did you?"

Adrienne Rich

Who ever thought up the word "Mammogram"? Every time I hear it, I think I'm supposed to put my breast in an envelope and send it to someone.

Jan King

The statistics are horrifying – now I can never be in a group of eight to ten women without thinking that one of us is likely to face this someday. It makes it very personal.

Cathy Guisewite on breast cancer

PAIN THRESHOLDS

Strictly speaking, there is but one real evil: I mean acute pain.

Lady Mary Wortley Montagu

Pain is a divine signal from heaven, nature, Mrs God, Mother Nature, whatever it is, telling us to mend our ways, to stop poisoning ourselves, to clean ourselves out.

Gloria Swanson

Illness is the night-side of life, a more onerous citizenship. Everyone who is born holds duel citizenship, in the kingdom of the well and in the kingdom of the sick.

Susan Sontag

The one thing that gets sympathy is a cry of pain – the reality of other people's bodies.

Pat Barker

I have a very low threshold of pain. Not even a limbo dancer could get down there.

Kathy Lette

People are too fond of pouring medicine into their bodies.

Caroline M. Hallett

They focus on symptoms, rather than pre-ven-tion … But I can understand, everybody wants a magic bullet to take care of anything they've got going on.

Grace Slick

Doctors and nurses are people who give you medicine until you die.

Deborah Martin

Some of my worst enemies have been doctors.

Rebecca West

Once you've cured this and cured that, if you're making money out of ill people you're going to have to produce more ill people to keep going.

Margaret Atwood

To put private enterprise into the idea of health care is a *heinous crime*! Much better, waste it! Let it be *frittered* away! Let a bunch of dopes *lose* it!

Fran Lebowitz

God's medicine is Fresh Air. People will not believe in it just because there is plenty of it to be had.

Caroline M. Hallett

The ultimate indignity is to be given a bedpan by a stranger who calls you by your first name.

Maggie Kuhn

One of the most difficult things to contend with in a hospital is that assumption on the part of the staff that because you have lost your gall bladder you have also lost your mind.

Jean Kerr

One has a greater sense of intellectual degradation after an interview with a doctor than from any human experience.

Alice James

Research shows that the common cold is … so common you wouldn't be out of line to call it a floozy.

Ellen DeGeneres

No one would be foolish enough to say an ulcer is contagious, but almost everybody who has an ulcer got it from somebody, usually a relative or business associate.

Ann Landers

It is pleasant to think of the pure delight of two million germs lost in me – all treating this undefiled temple as an hotel, brothel, battleground, see-saws on my heart, "I spy" among a hundred veins, or to whatever use their whims tempt them.

Lady Diana Cooper

One's back seems to be made of a membrane, like a bat's wing: this should be stretched tight, in order to deal adequately with the flight of existence; but suddenly it flops, and becomes (I imagine) like a veil which has fallen into a cup of tea.

Virginia Woolf

My entrails do their best to distract me from the suffering of my soul.

Julie Lespinasse

Please Don't Retouch
My Wrinkles

FORTY-SIX IS THE NEW THIRTY

Ladies scorn dates! Dates make ladies nervous and stories dry.

Harriette Wilson

All your age says about you is how long you've been alive.

Reverend Dianna Gwilliams

You need not flaunt your age in everybody's face. Practically everything about you is more interesting than the number of winters you have shivered through.

Renee Long

The years that a woman subtracts from her age are not lost. They are added to other women's.

Diane de Poitiers

Youth is an arithmetical statement of passing interest, each hour eats it up.

Stevie Smith

Youth is something very new – twenty years ago no one mentioned it.

Coco Chanel

When I was sixteen all I wanted was to look like a forty-year-old divorcee.

Jenny Eclair

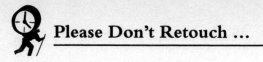

Please Don't Retouch ...

The really bad birthday I had was twenty-seven, because I knew that was the end of youth.

Joan Collins

At thirty, forty seemed not a decade but a century away.

Mariella Frostrup

At seventeen I longed to be twenty-five. At twenty I wanted to be a woman of the world of thirty. At thirty I read that the French thought a woman did not reach a full maturity of beauty and attractiveness until she was forty. Finally at forty-five, I decided that the whole thing was a pack of lies.

Mary Astor

I fought oestrogen tooth and nail.

Alice Walker

When I started, everyone said modelling only lasted five years. Yeah, right.

Jerry Hall

Forty isn't a dirty word for women any more.

Ira von Furstenberg

When I was forty, I used to wonder what people thought of me. Now I wonder what *I* think of them.

Brooke Astor at ninety-two

I was a buffoon and an idiot until the age of forty.

Madonna

Forty-six is the new thirty.

Gloria Estefan

The lovely thing about being forty is that you can appreciate twenty-five-year-old men more.

Colleen McCullough

I excessively hate to be forty. Not that I think it a bad thing to be — only I'm not ready yet!

Edith Wharton

Please Don't Retouch ...

What am I supposed to do until I'm old enough to play the Shirley MacLaine and Anne Bancroft parts? Go camping for ten years?

Cher

One day I said to myself: "I'm forty!" By the time I recovered from the shock of that discovery I had reached fifty.

Simone de Beauvoir

I refuse to admit that I am more than fifty-two, even if that does make my sons illegitimate.

Nancy Astor

I'm not prepared to subside into cronehood at fifty, I'm sorry.

Erica Jong

You have a choice, it seems to me, if you're middle-aged and single: believe the hype and take up macramé, or believe in yourself and get out there.

India Knight

You don't need to retire as an actor, there are all those parts you can play lying in bed, and in wheelchairs.

Judi Dench

There are those women who still like to look like students long into their thirties and forties, either because they haven't decided what to do with their lives yet, or their dotcom fortune never arrived. Oddly, it's little to do with mutton dressed as lamb, rather resilience got up like nostalgia.

Barbara Ellen

Prior to *The Golden Girls*, when old people were shown on television, you could almost smell them.

Bea Arthur

Since I have also now reached the age when I have positively not an eyelash of physical vanity left: my clackers can rattle down to my flat feet and my wig drop off in front of the howling mob for all I care.

Caitlin Thomas

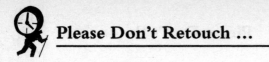
I've never really been the right age for what I've been doing.

Elaine Dundy

Seventy isn't old for a cathedral. But for a woman – ah, *mon Dieu* ...

Princess Pauline Metternich

I have always felt that a woman has the right to treat the subject of her age with ambiguity until, perhaps, she passes into the realm of over ninety. Then it is better she be candid with herself and with the world.

Helena Rubinstein

Please don't retouch my wrinkles. It took me so long to earn them.

Anna Magnani to a photographer

GENERATION GAPS

It's breathtaking how much people don't listen to the old.

Kate Millett

In the eyes of those twenty-year-olds, I see myself already dead and mummified.

Simone de Beauvoir

I can remember saying helpfully to a new-made widow, aged about thirty-five: "Never mind, you'll soon be dead, too."

Gwen Raverat

The dead might as well try to speak to the living as the old to the young.

Willa Cather

When I see a young girl I view her with the same pity that she views me with.

Lilli Palmer

When people regret the passing of their young days, I don't know what they are talking about. The embarrassment, heartache, and sense of insecurity which most young people suffer are surely the badlands of life.

Ilka Chase

Please Don't Retouch ...

The youth thing is getting old.

Debra Winger

I leave the great world to girls that know no better.

Lady Mary Wortley Montagu

I always liked very old people when they were clean.

Harriette Wilson

R. F. C. – Ready for Chrysanthemums.

Brigitte Bardot's name for anyone over thirty-five

It came into my head that youth was the only thing that the more it was out of sight the less it was out of mind.

Hester Thrale

THE EFFECTS OF TIME

Time has the same effect on the mind as on the face; the predominant passion and the strongest feature become more conspicuous from the others' retiring. The various views of life are abandoned from want of ability to pursue them, as the fine complexion is lost in wrinkles.

Lady Mary Wortley Montagu

Does one get wise as time passes on, or is it only that one's old folly goes out of fashion and looks as unbecoming as an antiquated ball-dress?

Geraldine Endsor Jewsbury

To my extreme mortification, I grow wiser every day.

Lady Mary Wortley Montagu

I'm enjoying getting older. I'm not quite as stupid as I used to be. But I feel like it sure went by quickly.

Tama Janowitz

It is entirely up to a woman how she ages.

Lilli Palmer

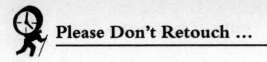

Please Don't Retouch ...

You want to look younger? Rent smaller children.

Phyllis Diller

If I get a grey hair and start to worry about it, I'll only get two more.

Grace Bumbry

Haven't you learned yet that it isn't age but lack of experience that makes us fall off ladders or have radiators fall on us?

Alice B. Toklas

I now find that age, when it does not harden the heart and sour the temper, naturally returns to the milky disposition of infancy.

Lady Mary Wortley Montagu

You always like to think that you got better with time.

Lillian Hellman

There were days last winter when I danced for sheer joy out in my frost-bound garden in spite of my years and children. But I did it behind a bush, having a due regard for the decencies.

Elizabeth von Arnim

One of the good things about living longer is that we have more time to learn *how* to be old.

Elizabeth Jane Howard

I don't remember the last time I felt anger. That will age you faster than anything.

Goldie Hawn

I have enjoyed greatly the second blooming that comes when you finish the life of the emotions and of personal relations; and suddenly find – at the age of fifty, say – that a whole new life has opened before you, filled with things you can think about, study, or read about … It is as if a fresh sap of ideas and thoughts was rising in you.

Agatha Christie

I often say "Every age has its happiness and its beauty." So my vanity finds words to console itself.

Liane de Pougy

I used to dread getting older because I thought I would not be able to do all the things I wanted to do, but now that I am older I find that I don't want to do them.

Nancy Astor

But old women are different from everybody else; they say what they think.

Ursula Le Guin

OUTLIVING YOUR BODY

Age to women is like Kryptonite to Superman.

Kathy Lette

It's the menopause. I've got my own climate.

Julie Walters

I have figured out the difference between a hot flash and a flashback. A flashback is when you can still hear Jerry Garcia. A hot flash is when you're just sweating like Jerry Garcia.

Diane Nichols

I've outlived most of my body, and I'm trying so hard – oh, God, I've had so many things done to my body, when I die God won't know me.

Phyllis Diller

The worst of old age is the tiredness. And the terrible *slowness* with which one does everything. Time goes at appalling speed and one has nothing to show for it.

Antonia White

With age, one tends to wrap one's misery around one, for fear that this last threadbare blanket will be taken away too.

Caitlin Thomas

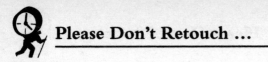

Please Don't Retouch …

Women are not like wine. They do not age better if left unnoticed and undisturbed.

Renee Long

As far as I'm concerned, old age brings no compensations whatsoever.

Lady Diana Cooper

The older I get the more difficult I find it is to be sporting.

Cornelia Otis Skinner

I've got enough crows' feet to start a bird sanctuary.

Kathy Lette

Like all human creatures, I am an interesting case. I apparently almost died, but did not … a failing but not sick heart. I am simply wearing out, like an old side-wind Victrola running down …

M. F. K. Fisher

When we next meet – I shall be tapping along Gloucester Road with a stick and a dog to lead me and a green shade over my eyes. You will give me a penny and say "Poor old creature, look Marny – she really is like that old goat we used to know."

Virginia Woolf

Your mind is a cantankerous old computer that doesn't always remember how to access the old files.

Marge Piercy

Remembering something at first try is now as good as an orgasm as far as I am concerned.

Gloria Steinem

Birthdays are nasty high-water marks. One just sees how far the tide has receded, and all the sand-banks on which one has a chance of getting stranded.

Geraldine Endsor Jewsbury

I hate time and its tyranny.

Edith Piaf

Please Don't Retouch ...

I blame Mother Nature (two-faced bitch!) and Father Time (bloody bastard!).

Kathy Lette

Melancholy ever attends upon the contemplation of transition, whether the transition relates to an external or an internal state, whether it involves progression or decay.

Harriet Martineau

Many people stop living before they are dead.

Renee Long

I haven't been funny for twenty years now.

Dorothy Parker

You can judge your age by the amount of pain you feel when you come in contact with a new idea.

Pearl S. Buck

The Ladies Have The Last Word

FROM LIFE TO DEATH

My dream is to die in a tub of ice cream, with Mel Gibson.

Joan Rivers

My favourite hobbies are reading, sex and sleeping, so death doesn't worry me; I imagine it to be a kind of deep sleep.

Olivia Goldsmith

With the newspaper strike on, I wouldn't consider dying.

Bette Davis, on being told that her death was rumoured

I am curious about it, that is, the actual act of dying, and I hope to be fully conscious and aware. Perhaps that is because I am a writer, although I feel fairly certain that there is no danger of my living to describe it.

M. F. K. Fisher

It bothers me that we've developed a culture that denies mortality and that so many are terrified of the end of life.

Claire Rayner

One might think that the scientific man of the twentieth century would have learned to deal with this uniform fear as successfully as he has been able to add years to his life span … [Yet] advancement of science has not contributed to but rather detracted from man's ability to accept death with dignity.

Elisabeth Kübler-Ross

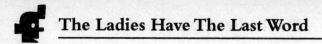

The Ladies Have The Last Word

Dear, this is the hardest bloody part I've ever played.

Eithne Dunne on her deathbed

School never ends. The classroom is everywhere. The exam comes at the very end.

Anna Quindlen

I love Death because he breaks the human pattern and frees us from pleasures too prolonged as well as from the pains of this world.

Stevie Smith

As you plunge into the rustling, rotting autumn of your life, it's only natural to turn towards the sun, whereas those young things in the springtime of their years seem to enjoy nothing more than spending all summer long lurking in a darkened bedroom listening to people singing about topping themselves. But death stops seeming like a hot date and more like a minging stalker the closer you get to him.

Julie Burchill

To be with a dying patient makes us conscious of the uniqueness of the individual in this vast sea of humanity, aware of our finiteness, our limited life span.

Elisabeth Kübler-Ross

I don't feel I do really belong to this life. I am hovering like a seagull.

Isak Dinesen

[The biological clock] is a murmur compared to the tolling of mortality.

Anna Quindlen

But one wants that idea of Death, you know, as something large and unknowable, something that allows a person to stretch himself out. Especially one wants it if one is tired.

Stevie Smith

Because I have loved life, I shall have no sorrow to die.

Amelia Burr

The Ladies Have The Last Word

The reason I don't fear death is that every chromosome of me is already in younger people.

Ellen Gilchrist

FUNERALS

This obvious discrepancy is the abortive drawback to funerals. They should be staged beforehand; so that at least the Corpse of Honour could join in the jubilating celebrations too. They are not staged for the dead, but for the living afterwards.

Caitlin Thomas

Italians and black people go crazy at the funerals. Irish people, they go crazy *after* the funeral.

Whoopi Goldberg

I think funerals are barbaric.

Mary Astor

In a churchyard the remains of humanity tell of the destinies of humanity, and thoughts of life and death rise as "by natural exhalation" from the ground we tread.

Harriet Martineau

It is appalling not to be there to console someone for the pain you cause by leaving him.

Simone de Beauvoir

The bitterest tears shed over graves are for words left unsaid and deeds left undone.

Harriet Beecher Stowe

For my epitaph, I think "Here lies one whose name is writ in Diet Coke" would be appropriate.

Olivia Goldsmith

Nothing is stronger than the position of the dead among the living.

Virginia Woolf

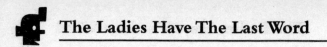

It's in your fifties that the first great harvesting begins of the friends. People your own age die and then it really gets serious.

Erica Jong

When friends die, one's own credentials change: one becomes a survivor.

Shirley Hazzard

LIFE AFTER DEATH

If I weren't cremated, I'd leave all the useful bits of my body to science – except my thighs because nobody would want those.

Olivia Goldsmith

The notion that the dead are asleep is mawkish, untrue and another cliché.

Germaine Greer

What can heaven be, that it could contain the infinite variety and pleasures of this earth?

Fay Weldon

I should very much like to know the sequel to our story.

Simone de Beauvoir

I'd been taught that when people died they went to Heaven, but I discovered as quickly that there was no possibility of going there alive. So if my mother died, I'd have to die too to be with her. This uncomfortable choice haunted me, at increasing intervals, for years.

Elizabeth Jane Howard

It is infamous the way most men in the world live and die, and are never missed, and, like us women, leave nothing but tombstones.

Isabel Arundell (later Burton)

God be thanked, I despise death.

Mary Queen of Scots, on the eve of her execution

The Ladies Have The Last Word

Death starts history and fears.

Gertrude Stein

Life without a body to put in it can't be much fun.

Caitlin Thomas

I think reincarnation is possible. Hopefully, we all get recycled.

Christina Ricci

I don't believe in God. Some days, I believe we all go into some
sort of central blender, like grass clippings.

Tama Janowitz

It is no good telling me that Hell is in the hereafter. For I am
prepared to swear that it is here on this bleeding Earth, and
nowhere else. And Heaven too.

Caitlin Thomas

Hell looks like the girls' gym at my high school. In hell, I am
taking gym, but I also have a book due.

Fran Lebowitz

I suppose we shall all come right in Heaven, as in a country dance
… all meet their partners when the jig is done.

Lady Mary Wortley Montagu

I wonder if we shall know each other in heaven, and whether we
shall be a chosen band as we are here.

Emily Dickinson

When I arrive at the pearly gates, I hope God says to me, "We've
reserved the penthouse suite for you and your friends are all
waiting."

Ina Garten

My heaven will be filled with wonderful young men and dukes.

Barbara Cartland

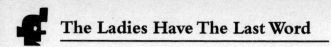

The Ladies Have The Last Word

Paradise is exactly like where you are right now … only much, much better.

Laurie Anderson

Life is better than death, I believe, if only because it is less boring, and because it has fresh peaches in it.

Alice Walker

Index

Index

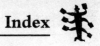

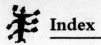

Index

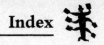

Index

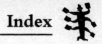

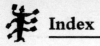

Index

Index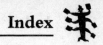

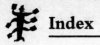

Index

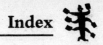

Index

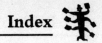

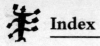

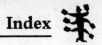

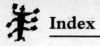

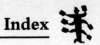

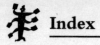

Index